Managing Water Supply and Sanitation in Emergencies

John Adams

Oxfam

First published by Oxfam GB in 1999

© Oxfam GB 1999

ISBN 0 85598 378 7

A catalogue record for this publication is available from the British Library.

Available from the following agents:
for the USA: Stylus Publishing LLC, PO Box 605, Herndon, VA 20172-0605, USA;
tel. +1 (0)703 661 1581; fax +1 (0)703 661 1501; email styluspub@aol.com
for Canada: Fernwood Books Ltd., PO Box 9409, Stn. A, Halifax, Nova Scotia B3K 5S3, Canada;
tel. +1 (0)902 422 3302; fax +1 (0)902 422 3179; email fernwood@istar.ca
for Southern Africa: David Philip Publishers, PO Box 23408, Claremont 7735, South Africa;
tel. +27 (0)21 64 4136; fax +27 (0)21 64 3358; email dpp@iafrica.com
for India: Maya Publishers Pvt Ltd, 113-B, Shapur Jat, New Delhi-110049, India;
tel. +91 (0)11 649 0451; fax +91 (0)11 649 1039
for Australia: Bush Books, PO Box 1370, Gosford South, NSW 2250, Australia;
tel. +61 (0)2 4323 3274; fax +61 (0)2 9212 2468; email bushbook@ozemail.com.au

For the rest of the world, contact Oxfam Publishing, 274 Banbury Road, Oxford OX2 7DZ, UK.
tel. +44 (0)1865 311 311; fax +44 (0)1865 313 925; email publish@oxfam.org.uk

Printed by Information Press, Eynsham, Oxford

Published by Oxfam GB, 274 Banbury Road, Oxford OX2 7DZ, UK

Oxfam GB is a registered charity, no. 202 918, and is a member of Oxfam International.

Contents

Acknowledgements

This book aims to present the combined wisdom of many people who have contributed text and comments. I hope it successfully reflects their rich and varied experience. In particular I should thank the following colleagues, currently or formerly employed by Oxfam GB, for their contributions: Andy Bastable, Donald Chaikin, Pat Diskett, Richard Luff, Woldu Mahary, Jean McClusky, Shona McKenzie, Lina Payne, Alan Reed, Catherine Robinson, Paul Sherlock, Paul Smith-Lomas, Sarah Totterdell, and many others whose ideas I have borrowed without asking.

A great deal of technical information was taken from the Technical Manuals that accompany Oxfam's water and sanitation equipment. Extensive reference is made to *Engineering in Emergencies* by Jan Davis and Bobby Lambert of RedR. Chapter 11 draws heavily on *Disease Prevention through Vector Control* by Madeleine Thomson, published by Oxfam in 1995. Chapter 6 was written jointly with Tom Corsellis of the University of Cambridge. Chapter 7 is based on Oxfam's unpublished Guidelines for Hygiene Promotion in Emergencies, written by Suzanne Ferron. Many other sources of information are included in the list of references and further reading. However, I take full responsibility for the present text.

Special thanks are due to Jan Davis for advice during the writing of the book, and for extensive comments on the final draft. I am grateful to my current employers, Community Aid Abroad – Oxfam Australia, for allowing me to take time off my work for them during the final stages of the project.

Last but not least, my thanks are due to Virginie for her forbearance during the writing of this book at home.

John Adams

Part 1 | Introduction

1 | Introduction

1.1 Purpose, contents, and scope of the book

1.1.1 Scope of the book

In emergency settlements, as in all vulnerable communities, health risks arising from contaminated water and poor sanitation, and the measures taken to reduce disease transmission are crucial determinants of the health and well-being of the population.

This book deals with water supply, excreta disposal, control of disease-transmitting vectors, hygiene promotion, solid-waste disposal, drainage, and selection and planning of settlements in emergency situations. It aims to provide an understanding of these programme elements, together with information and ideas for management and decision making in complex situations where both speed and good judgement are essential. The major focus of the book is water supply and sanitation, as this reflects Oxfam's main experience and current priorities in emergency-response work. Site selection and planning are included to reflect their links with water supply and sanitation, and because Oxfam[1] has had some experience in these fields in the past.

The book is divided into three parts. The first, *Introduction*, describes the range and evolution of emergency situations likely to be encountered, defines the health risks to be addressed by a water and sanitation project, and looks at needs and standards related to emergency water supply and sanitation. It describes features of a public-health approach to water supply and sanitation in emergencies, and discusses working with people affected by disasters. This part is aimed at all readers and sets the context for the rest of the book.

---

[1] 'Oxfam' in this book refers to Oxfam GB, based in Oxford, England.

The second part, *Programme Management,* concentrates on procedures and information needed for planning, implementing, monitoring, and evaluating water supply and sanitation projects. It includes sources of assessment information, advice on using health-related information for planning and response, and guidelines for monitoring, evaluation, and reporting, and for budget writing and project planning. The second half of this part covers procedures for managing the resources needed for project implementation, including personnel, logistics, and administration. This section is intended as a tool for general planning and decision making and is aimed at project and programme managers, including technical staff.

The third part, *Technical Chapters,* looks at each of the project areas, and gives practical guidance on planning and choosing technical options and putting them into practice. 'Technical', in this book, refers to specific aspects of hygiene promotion or vector control, as much as to pump installation or pipeline design. Each chapter begins with an introduction to the health and planning aspects of the subject. This part is intended primarily for technical staff who may need guidance on specific points, and for programme and project managers who are interested in developing their understanding of the technical issues. It does not provide comprehensive and detailed technical information, because this exists already in several other publications, including the Technical Manuals that are supplied with Oxfam's emergency water-supply and well-digging equipment.

This is not a book to be read from cover to cover. Different people may need to read different sections, and will not necessarily refer to them in the order in which they are presented. When using the book to help with programme design, for instance, it may be necessary to refer to Part 3 for ideas on technical options before turning to Part 2 for project planning.

1.1.2 Types of emergency considered

The book is based mostly on Oxfam's emergency experience over the past ten or so years, which has been dominated by population movements in Africa, resulting in camps of refugees or displaced people in rural surroundings. More recent and increasing experience in urban situations, often in colder climates, such as in Eastern Europe and the former Soviet Union countries, is reflected to a lesser extent. Advice and information concerning natural disasters relates to conditions prevailing some days after the event, when people are living in temporary settlements or the ruins of their homes. Many of the issues concerning camps of displaced people and refugees are relevant to this type of situation.

Many people affected by emergencies are not found in camps, but may stay with family and friends in towns and villages, or may be scattered in the countryside. Most of the health problems related to water and sanitation that are encountered in these situations are of far less importance than those encountered in large camps, and humanitarian agencies are less often involved in operational programmes in such circumstances. This book deals primarily with camps of at least 10,000 people, although there are sections which focus on other situations, such as refugees on the move or displaced people living in urban areas, and most of the principles and techniques discussed may be applied equally to small and transient settlements.

The following typology summarises the range of emergency situations in which Oxfam is involved, and which are addressed by this book. It is a typology of resulting emergency situations, rather than a review of their causes.

Large population movements along roads

Conditions: When large numbers of people move along a route, existing sources of water are likely to be inadequate, and effectively there will be no toilets. People may be very short of water, and may cook and sleep by the side of the road, where faecal contamination will be very intense. Health risks for local communities along the road may be significant. People may not be able to carry sufficient shelter materials to protect themselves from the elements. This situation rarely continues for more than a few days or weeks.

Programme considerations: Access may be restricted because of the number of people on the road. The location of priority needs changes daily as people move, so the response has to be flexible and mobile. It is important to provide information to people on the move about the location of water sources, resting and camping areas, health facilities, etc. Clearing faeces from the side of the road may be an important public-health measure, for local people as well as for the people on the move.

People displaced into scattered, transient, or seasonal settlements

Conditions: People may often settle in small family groups near major roads, and move from time to time. They may have carried their own shelter or may be able to find local shelter materials. Water supplies may be local springs or surface-water sources, leaks from water mains, or nearby treated supplies. There are unlikely to be any toilets. Support from local people and access to local services are unlikely. The people concerned may be habitually mobile.

Programme considerations: Usually only short-term or mobile technical solutions are possible, as people tend to move on. Implementation and monitoring may be difficult, because of the number of sites to cover and their impermanent nature. Community mobilisation may be very difficult.

People displaced into scattered, established settlements

Conditions: Some services are available, but they may not be sufficient for the added number of people. In many rural areas there are no toilets, or very few. People may stay with friends or relatives, or may be able to find local shelter materials. Local disease problems may be created or made worse by the arrival of displaced people, but large-scale epidemics are unlikely.

Programme considerations: Services provided are shared between local people and displaced people. Local people may have a long-term interest in improved water supplies and sanitation, but may be reluctant to invest in services that they have to share with displaced people.

People displaced into or within urban areas, staying in houses

Conditions: This depends very much on the wealth and condition of the communities hosting the displaced people. In poor areas, existing infrastructure is likely to be limited, houses overcrowded, and hygiene conditions poor. Because of this and because displaced people may bring new diseases with them, the incidence of water-related and sanitation-related disease and epidemics is high. Severe problems related to water, sanitation, and shelter provision may go unnoticed, because the displaced population is dispersed and there are no obvious and distinct groups of people in need.

Programme considerations: Common solutions for camps in rural areas may not be possible, because of the population density and the limits created by operating in an urban environment. On the other hand, it may be possible to reinforce local water supplies and sanitation services to meet increased need.

People displaced into urban areas, staying in public buildings or open spaces

Conditions: Existing shelter may be completely unsuitable for large numbers of people, and in cold climates may lack heating or weather-proofing. Water supplies and sanitation may be inadequate or completely absent. People may collect water from nearby houses, small numbers of public water points, or leaks in the distribution system. There may be open defecation in public spaces and along roads, with consequent health risks for local communities, as well as for displaced people. Displaced people may have security problems or uncertain legal or social status, which may be the reason why they do not stay with friends and relatives.

Programme considerations: There may be legal or social obstacles to improving public buildings or constructing shelters in open spaces. Some buildings may consist of several storeys, posing technical problems for water supplies and excreta disposal. Existing services may need strengthening, or it may be necessary to install separate services.

People displaced into large settlements (camps)

Conditions: Camps may be located and planned to provide minimum standards for a healthy and secure living environment. But unplanned camps may be overcrowded, with insufficient water supplies, sanitation facilities, and shelter materials. They may be in areas which are not settled by local people because of local disease risks such as malaria, or the risk of flooding.

Programme considerations: It may be uncertain how long the camp will remain, so long-term planning is difficult. Service provision may be cost-effective and rapid because of the concentrated settlement. On the other hand, many services might not have needed to be provided by an outside agency if the people were not in a camp. It is important to consider local impact.

People living briefly in transit centres or camps

Conditions: These centres often have fluctuating populations and may be overcrowded. There may be a high proportion of sick and weak people, and some may stay for some time before moving to a more permanent settlement. These centres are usually sited for easy access and may be highly managed by outside agencies. There is no long-term interest in the settlement among the people living there. The centre may be an established facility, such as a school or a football stadium.

Programme considerations: The short-term perspective suggests that it is not appropriate to invest in permanent infrastructure, unless the site is chosen for future use. Special care may be needed to avoid disease related to water supply and sanitation, because of the movement of people, the high proportion of vulnerable individuals, and conditions which may be overcrowded and unhygienic. Hygiene-promotion activities may be limited by the time available, but people's presence in the centre may be an opportunity for promoting hygiene practices that may be of benefit at the final destination.

People not displaced, but homes and infrastructure damaged by war or natural structural disaster

Conditions: Houses may be damaged or destroyed, and people may be exposed to severe conditions, particularly in cold winters or rainy periods. Water supplies and sewers may be damaged or destroyed, and broken sewers may contaminate living areas and water supplies. Access may be cut in rural areas, and in urban areas damaged buildings may block streets.

Programme considerations: Short-term and long-term housing repairs may be needed, and some people may require temporary accommodation. Temporary power supplies may be needed for restoring water supplies, with isolation of damaged water mains and sewers. In some settlements there may be traditional water supplies that are less affected and which can be used. Access to the community via established health and administrative structures is easier than in displaced settlements.

Local displacement due to natural disaster

Conditions: People may be forced by floods to move to higher ground, or forced by the threat or event of volcanic eruption to move to safer areas. Ground-water supplies may be contaminated by floodwater, or water-supply infrastructure and sanitation facilities may be damaged by storms or earthquakes. Crops and other means of livelihood may be destroyed. People may often be able to move back to their homes after a short space of time in temporary accommodation.

Programme considerations: Short-term assistance may be needed in temporary sites for displaced people. Contaminated wells, collapsed latrines, and blocked drainage and sewer systems may need rehabilitation, with short-term measures taken for water supplies and sanitation. Houses may need repair or replacement. Vector control may be a priority if stagnant water remains for some time after the floods occur, or if drainage channels are damaged. A large volume of debris may need removing.

1.1.3 Definitions

For the purposes of this book, the following definitions are used.

- *Disaster:* A situation where people's normal means of life support with dignity have failed as a result of natural or man-made catastrophe.
- *Disaster-affected people:* People affected by a disaster, including refugees, internally displaced people, and people affected by war or natural disaster who remain at or near their homes. Also, people indirectly affected by the disaster, such as a community hosting a displaced population.
- *Disaster mitigation:* Work to ensure that disasters, if and when they strike, have less impact. In other words, reducing vulnerability so that individuals, families, and communities are better able to withstand and recover from disasters.
- *Disaster preparedness:* Planning and preparing to react to disasters, on the basis of an assessment of risk, vulnerabilities, and likely responses needed; making contacts with likely key actors, and acquiring basic practical information that would be required in the event of a response.
- *Emergency settlement:* Any settlement where disaster-affected people may be, whether it is a refugee camp, a communal building, or people's own homes.
- *Environmental health:* Health matters relating to risks of disease in the living and working environment, such as water-borne and air-borne disease.
- *Epidemiology:* Used in this book to describe public-health surveillance, or the regular collection and analysis of quantitative information about health for programme decisions, as well as the investigation of disease patterns during or after specific outbreaks of disease.
- *Project:* All planned water-supply and sanitation interventions, whether they consist of a single activity, such as distributing water containers, or a set of related activities within the water supply, sanitation, and hygiene-promotion sector. Where the word *programme* is used, this refers to a broader set of projects, which may include nutrition, health services, social services, etc.

- *Public health:* Health matters affecting the whole of the population concerned, including environmental health matters.
- *Risk:* Risk of disaster occurring.
- *Vulnerability:* Lack of protection against disasters when they strike. Vulnerability operates at many different levels, from individuals through families and communities to countries. The more vulnerable people are, the more severely affected by the disaster they are likely to be, and/or less able to recover from the disaster.

1.2 Environmental health risks in emergencies

The health risks posed by disasters may include one or several of the following: personal injury through conflict or natural disaster; loss of livelihoods and shortage of resources such as food and clothing; damage to services such as water supply and health care; fatigue, hunger, and disease due to flight in difficult and dangerous conditions; stress and trauma; and the excessive concentration of people in unfamiliar and often overcrowded and dirty conditions. These may cause considerable physical and psychological harm in the long term, as well as during the emergency period.

The two most important *environmental health* risks in most emergency situations are insufficient and unsafe water, and inadequate excreta disposal. Other risks, such as disease-transmitting vectors (mosquitoes, rats, flies, etc.), poor drainage, and inadequate shelter and clothing are frequently significant; others, such as toxic waste, may themselves be the main feature of the emergency. Together, the different risks related to environmental health may account for most cases of sickness and death in the affected population, unless rapid and effective action is taken. Whatever the health risks and the actions taken to reduce them, the ultimate impact on health is moderated by people's own hygiene-related behaviour.

Excreta-related disease
A major cause of sickness and death among refugees is excreta-related disease. There are a number of routes by which disease-causing organisms contained in excreta, or related to them, may be transmitted, but the most important are by ingesting faeces (the faeco-oral route), and by contaminated hands, food, and water. It is by these routes that diseases such as diarrhoeas (including cholera), shigella, hepatitis, and typhoid fever are transmitted. Other excreta-related transmission routes involve soil-transmitted parasite worms (helminths), such as roundworm (ascaris) and hookworm, which develop in the soil after being excreted by infested humans; beef and pork tapeworms, transmitted when cattle or pigs ingest infested human excreta; water-based helminths, such as bilharzia (schistosomiasis); and disease-carrying vectors such as certain mosquitoes which breed in heavily contaminated water, and flies, which may be involved in transmitting certain diarrhoeal diseases.

Water-related disease

Many of the most important excreta-related diseases are, because of their transmission through drinking water, also water-related. In this sense, clean water supply is a secondary barrier to many infectious diseases. By providing water that is of sufficient quantity to enable people to wash themselves, and particularly their hands, of excreta, and of sufficient quality to eliminate or avoid the water-borne transmission route, most of the important excreta-related diseases can be avoided, provided that people practise good hygiene. In some situations absolute lack of drinking water may cause disease and death from dehydration, particularly among people affected by diarrhoea.

In some conditions, surface water may provide breeding sites for disease-carrying insect vectors and for the intermediate hosts of diseases such as schistosomiasis and guinea-worm infestation.

Other diseases related to environmental health

Other diseases related to environmental health include those encouraged by overcrowding and inadequate shelter, such as respiratory infections, measles, and diseases borne by lice and fleas. Noise, overcrowding, heat, cold, and lack of privacy all add to stress and ultimately to poor health. Some disasters, such as chemical accidents, may cause direct environmental health risks. These problems demand a highly specialised response and are not discussed in this book.

1.3 Needs and standards

Needs for basic resources such as potable water or toilets may vary according to many factors such as climate, culture, and the nature of the emergency. An assessment of needs should be the basis of any response involving emergency water supply and sanitation. Minimum standards for the delivery of humanitarian assistance in the areas of water supply and sanitation, sites and shelter, food aid, nutrition and health services have been developed by a number of agencies through the Sphere Project on Minimum Standards in Humanitarian Response. Each of the standards is supported by a set of key indicators, to help to set objectives, and to plan and measure the effectiveness of the response. The standards provide a description of what disaster-affected people have a right to expect from humanitarian assistance. They reflect agencies' commitment to fundamental humanitarian principles and the rights of disaster-affected people under international law. At the time of writing, these standards are being field-tested and verified, to ensure that they are applicable and useful in a wide range of disasters, and to provide guidance on their use in practice. The standards formalise the level of service that disaster-affected people should expect. This level of service will not be possible in all situations, and will take time to achieve, even in the most favourable circumstances. Therefore a flexible approach, informed by principles of public health, should be used to ensure that priorities are met and that life and health are protected at each stage of the disaster response.

The Sphere standards are frequently referred to in this text, and staff working on water-supply and sanitation projects should be familiar with the relevant sections, particularly Chapters 1 and 2. See 'Further reading' at the end of this chapter.

1.4 Public-health approach to water supply and sanitation in emergencies

1.4.1 Features of a public-health approach

A public-health approach to water supply and sanitation in emergencies is distinguished by four major features: a reliance on public-health information for managing the response; a co-ordinated response; a response aimed at maximum impact on the health of the affected population as a whole; and a dynamic — or phased — response, which adapts to meet changing needs over time.

Information-based response
A public-health intervention is made on the basis of recent, relevant, and reliable information about the health and health-related situation of the population concerned. There needs to be an appropriate strategy for collection and careful interpretation of such information, in order to adapt activities to meet public-health priorities, such as a diarrhoea epidemic or a malaria outbreak. Information is continually gathered to monitor the impact of the programme on health. These health-related data, which are gathered from all sectors, interpreted, and used for decision making, are often called a Health Information System, which is an important tool for co-ordination. See section 4.1 on monitoring. Even at the outset of an emergency, when accurate data may not be available, decisions about public health are made on the basis of the best information available at the time. See section 1.4.2 below.

Population-based response
An effective public-health intervention in an emergency concentrates both on producing the widest possible impact as quickly as possible (for instance, aiming to produce a minimum quantity of water for all within a few days), and on identifying and reaching groups of people who are particularly in need or who are at risk of being excluded (for instance, ensuring that a minority group at the edge of the settlement is given adequate access to the taps, that facilities provided are suitable for people with specific disabilities, or that women have safe and convenient access to facilities).

To ensure that the needs of all people in the affected community are considered, data should be disaggregated according to age, gender, ethnicity, and types of disability at the earliest opportunity. Vulnerability is determined greatly by poverty and lack of family or other support mechanisms, so an understanding of who in the community is most poor and most unsupported will ensure a more sensitive response. See also section 1.7 on social diversity.

Co-ordinated response
Once priorities are established on the basis of public-health information, actions need to be co-ordinated to ensure that priorities are met and programmes adapted as the situation changes. Although, in practice, different agencies often take responsibility for different aspects of the programme, their activities are linked, both epidemiologically and operationally, and these links should be recognised and managed in order to ensure success. For instance, an agency managing a latrine-construction programme has to be aware of the location of wells planned by the water-supply agency, to be able to avoid locating latrines too close to the wells, with the risk of contaminating them. Staff running the hygiene-promotion programme need clear information from the water-supply programme, in order to inform the population of developments in the water-supply system and to help them to arrange controlled and fair access to water points, if water is scarce.

Co-ordination is needed between programme areas, as well as within the water and sanitation sector. Disasters affect the health and lives of people in many ways, and interventions are needed in several areas to safeguard health, life, and livelihoods. Food supplies, sanitation, water supply, health care, health education, and security are all indispensable and inter-linked components of the overall response. For the most effective impact on public health, these components are integrated by effective inter-agency co-ordination or by one agency taking responsibility for several related sectors. In most large emergencies, there is a UN body charged with co-ordinating the efforts of the various relief agencies involved, in collaboration with government departments. The larger the number of different organisations that are present, the harder the co-ordination role becomes, and the more important it is. Integrating all the elements of a public-health programme is a difficult task in practice, but it does increase the chance that priority actions are identified and carried out, and that the programme is able to adapt as priorities change.

Dynamic (or phased) response
For the maximum impact on health, interventions should focus on immediate problems as well as longer-term objectives. Emergencies are dynamic events, and programmes should take account of this. The problems which arise and the responses needed to address them are not the same immediately after disaster as they will be six months later. The response should aim to meet urgent needs and give time for planning and organising longer-term solutions, building, where possible, on equipment used during the first stage. A loose definition of phases with appropriate types of water supply and

sanitation response is given in Chapter 3, section 2. The phases may be called **acute emergency** (first phase), **stabilised emergency** (second phase), and **post-emergency** (third phase). There is no time scale given for these phases, because passing from one to the next depends very much on factors such as the performance of the agencies, political events, population movements, and occurrence of epidemics. Some situations move from a stable phase to an acute phase as the result of epidemics, food shortages, or unrest in the camp. Annual cholera epidemics in the Mozambican refugee camps in Malawi during the late 1980s and early 1990s created first-phase conditions and demanded renewed first-phase action. Situations may remain in a state of chronic emergency for years, turning into acute emergencies from time to time, as is the case for many in southern Sudan.

Activities undertaken during the early stages of an emergency response should be seen as steps on the way to meeting minimum standards. There is no evidence to suggest that needs are somehow less during the early stages of an emergency than later on. It is important to try to close the gap between needs and services provided, quickly and effectively.

1.4.2 Health information for water-supply and sanitation programmes

Mortality rates

The overall public-health situation in a disaster-affected population is commonly described by the **crude mortality rate** (CMR), often expressed in emergency situations as the number of deaths per 10,000 people per day. The following benchmarks for evaluating the seriousness of the situation are now widely accepted.

0.5 per 10,000 per day: 'normal', or background rate for poor countries
<1.0 per 10,000 per day: under control
>1.0 per 10,000 per day: very serious situation
>2.0 per 10,000 per day: out of control
>5.0 per 10,000 per day: catastrophic

The benchmark mortality rates for under-fives (<5MR), expressed as deaths of children under the age of five per 10,000 children per day, are approximately double those of the CMR.

The CMR gives a very general measure of the health of the population concerned, but does not say anything about the reason why people are getting sick and dying, or who is most affected by health problems. Nor does it indicate a health problem until people start to die. For these reasons, it is important to try to get health information which gives specific causes of death (cause-specific mortality rate), which will give an indication of areas which need attention; specific causes of disease (cause-specific morbidity rate), which allows a response to a health problem to be mounted before deaths result; and data for morbidity and mortality which are disaggregated by age, sex, and location, to enable a response to be mounted which responds to problems faced by specific sectors of the population at risk.

Morbidity rates

Morbidity is usually expressed as a **prevalence**, i.e. the number of people in the population concerned who are suffering from a particular disease at any one time, for instance the percentage of the population with scabies; and **incidence**, or the number of new cases of a specific disease within the population concerned, over a specified time period, for instance cases of diarrhoea per 1,000 people per week.

An assessment of the seriousness of a specific disease problem is influenced by an understanding of the background morbidity rate, or expected morbidity rate, for a specific location or population. This recognises that a certain level of disease is inevitable, and suggests that programmes should aim to keep disease below certain levels, rather than to eliminate them completely. The definition of background or normal disease levels is done by looking at normal rates for the surrounding population, or for the affected population before the disaster, allowing for seasonal variations. It may be that the population was suffering an unusually high level of morbidity before the disaster, so an improvement in health from the 'normal' situation may be needed.

Endemic and epidemic morbidity rates

A disease pattern may be **endemic**, where a disease has been present for many years and where a 'normal' morbidity rate is established; or **epidemic**, where there is a rapid increase in disease incidence within the population, due to the introduction of a new disease or due to seasonal variations in transmission of or susceptibility to the disease. Thus malaria, which may be endemic in an area, may cause an epidemic among a non-immune population arriving from another area, or may cause seasonal epidemics at the start of the rainy season in an agricultural community as the number of mosquitoes increases and this coincides with malnutrition-related low immunity.

An endemic disease pattern is localised but long-term. An epidemic disease pattern is localised and relatively short-term, and is defined as an excessive number of cases of a given disease, in relation to prior experience, according to place, time, and population. So it is not possible to suggest widely applicable rates above which a disease incidence is defined as epidemic. In practice it is often difficult to make comparisons with previous years, and a judgement is made, according to the disease concerned, about the epidemic risk posed by the occurrence of a certain number of cases. Thus one case of cholera in a crowded refugee camp may be enough to declare an epidemic.

Reliability of health data

When using morbidity and mortality data for making decisions about water and sanitation provision, one should be aware of possible sources of error. Figures may be under-reported or over-reported for a variety of reasons, such as low attendance at health centres, inaccurate diagnosis, or mistakes in recording and transferring information. The most critical figure, the total population number, is very often highly unreliable. See section 4.1 for more on monitoring information.

1.5 Partners in the humanitarian response

Disaster-affected people
The people affected by a disaster provide their own first source of assistance, and the contribution of the other partners should be complementary to their efforts. Disaster-affected people may be **refugees**, who have crossed an international border to seek refuge in a host country, with special status and rights. They may be **displaced people**, who have fled from conflict or local disaster, but have not crossed an international boundary and are not usually offered the same assistance and protection; they may be worse off than refugees in many ways, particularly if their own government is hostile or simply indifferent to them. Refugees and displaced people may remain in need of outside assistance for some years, if they are unable to return to their homes because of continuing conflict or persecution.

Many people affected by conflict choose not to flee, or are unable to do so, but may suffer greatly from the direct and indirect effects of the conflict. People affected by acute natural disasters such as volcanic eruptions or floods are less likely to move far from home and may be able to rely more on local support. Those affected by so-called slow-onset emergencies such as drought and famine may be forced to move far from their homes and live in towns or camps, dependent to some extent on outside assistance.

One often refers to 'refugee communities', but there are many factors which divide people in emergencies, and in extreme cases all semblance of community may appear to break down, as individuals and families struggle for their own survival. Nevertheless, people do form or re-form communities in most cases, and it is important to recognise community structures and relations, to ensure that programmes reach those most in need and that they are carried out in a way that strengthens the most vulnerable or least powerful. Refugee communities may be extremely diverse, socially and economically, including a cross-section of a whole society, such as the Kurdish refugees who fled Iraq in 1991; or they may be formed of people with a generally similar background, such as the Mozambican refugees in some of the camps in Malawi during the late 1980s and early 1990s, who were mostly peasant farmers. Health problems related to water and sanitation are influenced by the mix of people affected by the disaster, and the various measures needed will depend on the vulnerability of different groups.

The local population
The local population and local community-based organisations may provide the first assistance to the disaster-affected people, before any outside agencies become aware of the situation and formally involved. Throughout the response, local people are involved as staff and providers of resources and information.

Host authorities
Host authorities are legally responsible for the protection and welfare of people affected by disasters within their territory. They are directly involved in the humanitarian response, as operational agencies or in a co-ordinating or regulating role. Local and regional health and engineering staff may work directly on water supply and sanitation programmes.

Humanitarian agencies
Humanitarian agencies have a role to play where local capacities are insufficient to meet the needs of the disaster-affected population, or where for other reasons sufficient local assistance is not provided. These organisations include inter-government organisations (IGOs), such as UNHCR, UNICEF, and WFP; international NGOs (INGOs); local NGOs (LNGOs); and the Red Cross/ Red Crescent organisations: the ICRC and IFRC with their national Societies. Local religious institutions may also be effective providers of assistance, with their local knowledge and influence.

1.6 Working with disaster-affected people

Oxfam has a commitment to working with people affected by disasters, to help in a collaborative way rather than taking all the decisions and implementing programmes without consultation and participation. Working *with* people affected by emergencies, rather than simply *for* them, is a policy with an ethical basis, but it is also a powerful tool for an effective public-health response and is essential for supporting dignity and recovery. Working *with* people also ensures that responses are culturally appropriate; it provides opportunities for social change, for instance, by allowing women to participate in decision making, perhaps for the first time in their lives. This approach involves developing relationships, sharing information and ideas vital for health, sharing decision making and power, and sharing the workload and responsibility for project implementation.

Working with people, or community participation, may imply any or all of the following measures:

- giving people the knowledge and/or resources to practise good hygiene and sanitation, given the constraints of the situation in which they find themselves: an element of *hygiene promotion;*

- consulting people on the direction and approach of the programme and listening to their ideas about the design, progress, and impact of the programme: *participatory assessment, planning, and evaluation;*
- training and skills transfer to help to build capacity for the emergency phase and possible return or resettlement; hygiene promotion is an important element of this *capacity building;*
- involving people as volunteers in the implementation of emergency measures and construction programmes: this is what is commonly understood by *community mobilisation.* Care is needed to ensure that the burden of work created by community mobilisation does not fall too heavily on the community as a whole, or on certain people who carry out tasks such as looking after water points or cleaning toilets.

Capacity building

This concept has specific applications in disasters, which have a lot to do with vulnerability and loss of capacity. One of the most basic types of capacity building is hygiene promotion: providing the information that people need to survive in an emergency. But camp situations in particular also provide opportunities for training for community health workers, water and sanitation committees, and ordinary people in simple health-related skills such as first aid or latrine construction. Rwandan refugees fleeing the Kivu camps towards Kisangani, Zaire in 1996 and 1997 were in some cases able to organise basic water supplies and sanitation, drawing on their experience in the Kivu camps over two years. Refugees returning to Mozambique from Malawi after 1992 quickly built latrines as they resettled. Most of their neighbours who had not been refugees did not.

Resettlement and post-emergency work

A refugee or displacement situation may result in people returning home at some stage (for example, Kurdish people returning to Iraq from Turkey and Iran in 1991); or they may remain in camps for very long periods (such as the Palestinian camps); or they may settle, either in concentrated settlements or rural areas, and establish livelihoods and become integrated into the local society and systems (as, for instance, Rwandan refugees who settled in Uganda from the 1960s). The agencies involved in the emergency response and subsequent work should be aware that sooner or later their involvement is likely to be much reduced or to cease altogether, as the camps disperse or as they hand over to local authorities and community organisations. The sustainability of systems and structures depends very much on the way in which they are designed. However, managers, engineers, and extension staff have an important role to play to ensure a positive long-term benefit.

Issues to consider when working with people in practice

It is important to consider ways of involving people, the different levels and types of involvement possible, and an appropriate schedule. During the early days of an emergency there may be many factors working against participation, such as the need to provide services immediately; the trauma that many people will have suffered, which makes it hard for them to get involved in participatory programmes; a feeling among refugees that they are not staying long; and the profile of the agency in a situation where there may be many different agencies trying to run similar programmes, with inadequate co-ordination. But if there is a commitment to participation, then the processes and activities leading towards it can start from the beginning of the programme. Otherwise participation will become increasingly difficult, as the relationship between the agency and the population served develops into one of provider and beneficiary.

1.7 Social diversity

Disaster-affected communities are socially diverse, as are all societies. Women and men have different roles and often have an unequal share of power and control of resources; older people have different status and needs from younger people; young children have special needs; disabled people may be particularly vulnerable and need particular facilities or care; richer families may be able to cope much better than poorer families. Managers should seek to recognise the social diversity of the communities affected by disasters and make efforts to ensure that this diversity is taken into account when planning and implementing a response.

The checklist below may help to ensure that the needs and concerns of all sections of the community are taken into account in assessments, implementation, training, and staffing, so that water and sanitation projects tend to encourage positive social changes, rather than reinforcing unfair social relations. Each of the following points may be used to check sensitivity to social diversity, including factors such as gender, poverty, disability, and age.

Assessment and planning

■ Are data on the use of and needs for water and sanitation collected for each sector of the community?

■ Are morbidity and mortality data differentiated according to social sectors?

■ Is social and economic information about the affected population disaggregated by social sectors?

■ What are the projected benefits or negative consequences of the programme for each sector of the community?

Accessibility and acceptance

- Are the work patterns, time uses, and preferences of each social sector taken into account when deciding on the placement of water systems and latrines, the timing of water operations, and the provision of training and education activities?
- Are the technologies used suitable for all groups in the community?
- Are health activities suitable and appropriate for all groups?

Project training

- Do training activities give equal opportunities to all groups?
- Does the promotional material portray people exclusively in traditional roles?

Project personnel

- Are there equal employment opportunities for all sectors of the community?
- Are people given the opportunity and training (where possible) to take on roles not traditionally considered appropriate?
- Are there situations where it is appropriate or necessary for certain positions to be socially specific?

The most vulnerable people affected by disasters may be very difficult to work with, for a number of reasons. Their leaders may not be truly representative and may present a view of the situation that suits their particular interests, or those of the more powerful, and they may effectively block contacts with certain sections of the community. Women may find it hard to participate in programmes because of their heavy workload, and this may demand special efforts and close liaison with the men, to enable them to join in decision making. Staff may lack the resources and techniques needed for communicating with a cross-section of diverse communities, and the need to act quickly may deter staff from taking the time to talk with people. There may also be a prevailing sense among many of the people responsible for the humanitarian response that it is not efficient to spend time consulting with disaster-affected people, when solutions seem relatively clear and can be managed without consultation.

It is important to assess the degree to which it is possible and desirable to work closely with the affected community before making programme decisions which depend on a certain level of participation. This assessment should consider the issues raised above and should involve discussion with members of the community and not rely on assumptions made by outsiders about people's capacity to act for themselves.

1.8 The local context

The emergency itself, the activities of refugees and displaced people, and the work of relief agencies all affect the economy, society, and environment of surrounding areas.

The local economy
There are often opportunities to provide employment and other economic opportunities for people living near emergency settlements. On the other hand, the disaster-affected population may compete for work and local business activity and they are often able to undercut local people, if they receive free food and free access to services, such as improved and maintained water supplies.

Local society
The presence of the disaster-affected community may have a big impact on surrounding communities, and relations between the two may have a strong influence on the environment in which agencies operate. There are many cases of local hostility expressed towards international agencies that focus solely on emergency work with a displaced or refugee population, and which do not pay sufficient attention to local needs and the local impact of the emergency. Programmes may influence forces for conflict or peace, both within the disaster-affected community and with local people, in a number of ways, including recruitment and payment practices, or use of and access to local water resources — see below. The relationship between emergency work and longer-term developments has to be carefully managed.

Services
The arrival of large numbers of refugees is likely to put a strain on local resources such as water supplies. This may cause hardship among local people, which may, in turn, lead to conflict. Emergency programmes should aim to ensure that local people's water supplies are safeguarded by providing additional supplies for the disaster-affected community as soon as possible. In many cases local water supplies are inadequate anyway, and there are opportunities to provide supplies for communities near refugee camps, and to design facilities which can be of use after temporary settlements have closed.

Health
Emergency settlements may pose a health risk to the surrounding population and vice versa, particularly in the case of epidemics such as cholera and shigella. Efforts should be made to protect surrounding communities by avoiding contamination of their water supplies, promoting good hygiene at markets where local people may come to trade, and generally working to establish a healthy environment in the settlement. Other important factors are access to health care for local people and the impact of the disaster-affected population on local health services.

The environment

Many disasters occur in areas that are environmentally important or fragile, and their environmental impact may be very great. This will have consequences for the livelihoods and health of local people and the sustainability of the emergency settlement, as well as for the economic and intrinsic value of the habitats affected. Although environmental concerns, which may have long-term significance, are difficult to balance against immediate human needs, careful judgements need to be made early on in the response, particularly concerning the location and size of settlements, in order to reduce costly and damaging environmental impact. It may happen that the disaster and the emergency response affect the vulnerability of local communities to future disasters. Responses should be designed and implemented in such a way that they reduce vulnerability, rather than increase it.

Further reading

S. Cairncross and R. Feachem (1993) *Environmental Health Engineering in the Tropics: An introductory text*, second edition, Chichester: John Wiley & Sons

J. Davis and R. Lambert (1995) *Engineering in Emergencies: A practical guide for relief workers*, Chapter 7, London: RedR/IT Publications

C. Mears and S. Chowdhury (1994) *Health Care for Refugees and Displaced People*. Oxford: Oxfam

MSF (1997) *Refugee Health: An approach to emergency situations*, London and Basingstoke: Médecins sans Frontières/Macmillan

Sphere Project (forthcoming, 1999) *Humanitarian Charter and Minimum Standards in Disaster Response*, published in Geneva by the Steering Committee for Humanitarian Response (SCHR) and Interaction; e-mail: sphere@ifrc.org; internet: *www.sphereproject.org*

Part 2 | Programme Management

2 | Assessment

2.1 Purpose

A good initial assessment is one of the keys to a successful emergency water-supply and sanitation project. It should enable some or all of the following:

- an initial decision to be made on whether assistance is needed at all;
- a decision to be made on whether local capacity is adequate or external resources are required;
- priorities for intervention to be established, including identifying the most vulnerable groups;
- a strategy for intervention to be identified;
- required resources to be identified;
- base-line data to be collected, to facilitate monitoring;
- information for fund-raising and advocacy work to be collected;
- potential partners to be identified: for example, government departments, local and international NGOs, and UN bodies.

While initial assessments are important for early decision making, assessment should not be seen as a one-off activity, but one that is used regularly to update and clarify the understanding of a situation.

2. 2 Sources of information

2.2.1 Existing information

Existing information may be available from many sources, including the following: satellite data, geographical information, rainfall, soil, and geological maps, and aerial photographs. These can provide a lot of background information on land use, terrain, vegetation, soil, water resources, etc., but this kind of information is not always easy to obtain at the time it is needed. Other agencies, government departments, universities, consultants, and contractors may have reports relevant to the situation, from field assessments, projects, or desk studies. Background information from these sources can be vital in helping to plan and implement any possible response, and it may be sufficient for preparing an outline plan of action, but there is no substitute for a field visit for up-to-date and verifiable information.

2.2.2 Field-assessment checklist

However experienced the field assessors are, and however well developed their intuitive understanding of emergency situations, it is helpful to use checklists for assessments. This ensures that all the relevant questions are asked, and that information is gathered, reported, and communicated in a structured form, and analysed to facilitate decision making. The checklist in Table 2.1 may be useful for carrying out an assessment of water-supply and sanitation needs and priorities in an emergency.

Table 2.1 Checklist for field assessment of water-supply and sanitation needs in emergencies

Questions	Sources of information	Comments
Background		
General assessment of context, including international, national, and local politics	Agency's past experience and reports; country briefing papers; Internet, etc.	This assessment may be the responsibility of a water and sanitation specialist, if nobody else from the agency is available to do it.
Demography and health		
How many people are involved? What are their likely movements? Are numbers likely to increase or decrease?	Official sources; camp managers; health staff; rapid counts and sample surveys; immunisation and nutrition surveys	Figures are likely to be very rough at this stage and to change rapidly. Keep them up to date and cross-check them with figures from different sources.
Are there many cases of diarrhoea and other diseases related to environmental health? If so, how are they distributed, geographically and by age group?	Health staff; home visits; a walk across a defecation field	See 1.2.
Are there epidemics within the population, in the area, or does the area experience seasonal epidemics?	Health staff and services; home visits; previous reports	The main causes of concern related to water and sanitation are epidemics of cholera, shigella, dysentery, other diarrhoeas, and malaria.

Table 2.1 Checklist for field assessment of water-supply and sanitation needs in emergencies (continued)

Questions	Sources of information	Comments
Demography and health (continued)		
What is the general state of health of the population? Are there nutritional problems? Are there many old or sick people? Have people travelled very far?	Health staff; home visits; local health services in the area; reports from local health services in area of origin (for displaced people)	Experience may help, but try to find hard evidence from health specialists.
What proportions of the population are men, women, and children? What proportions are pregnant women, unaccompanied children, elderly people?	Health staff; sample surveys; camp managers	This information may be very hard to obtain, but may be available from nutrition or vaccination surveys, even if a census has not been carried out.
Are data on mortality available? Is it possible to calculate a daily rate? If so, is this rate disease-specific?	Health staff; camp managers; graveyard statistics	See 1.4.2 for a discussion of mortality rates. Deaths may be heavily under-reported or (less often) over-reported.
Is a map of the site available?	Other workers; previous reports e.g. from government departments or military; rapid site survey	Maps are a basic tool for public-health and engineering work in camps. Even your own roughest sketch will help you to understand and plan. See Chapter 6.
Names of key informants, opinion leaders Household sizes Community organisation and structures (women's groups, water committees, religious institutions, social societies, youth groups, schools, health services, etc.) Existing outreach workers (community health workers, social development extension agents, etc.)	Local government; camp managers; health staff; distribution agencies; religious and social leaders; social or anthropological workers; development agencies	It is very important to understand what human resources are available within the affected community, in order to plan and implement programmes that are rapid, appropriate, and cost-effective, and which support local capacity.

Table 2.1 Checklist for field assessment of water-supply and sanitation needs in emergencies (continued)

Questions	Sources of information	Comments
Water supplies		
What water sources are being used now, and where exactly do the people collect the water?	Visits to water sources; asking water collectors; home visits	Where staff and time are available, it may be useful to record the number of people and animals coming to collect water at water points, and note how much each is collecting during a whole day.
How much water is available per person per day?	Visits to water sources and measurements of flow rates and volume of standing water; asking water collectors; home visits	As above. Look for signs of overnight queues, such as fires near the water source. Fix depth gauge in standing water to assess rate of abstraction.
How far do people have to go to collect water?	Site visits and walking to sources; asking water collectors; home visits	Measure time as well as distance. Estimate how long it takes to walk up a steep hill with a full bucket. Are there obstacles between shelters and water source?
Do people have enough water containers of the right size and type for collection and storage?	Water collectors; home visits	Questions like this could be included in other household surveys, such as nutrition surveys.
Do they have the means to use the water effectively for personal and domestic hygiene?	Home visits; health staff	Soap and additional water containers may be needed.
Is the water source being contaminated or at risk from contamination (microbiological and chemical/radiological)?	Visit to water sources for sanitary inspection and possibly microbiological testing	Use a sanitary survey form. See Chapter 8 for information on water quality and potential contamination.
Should and can protection of the water source be improved?	Visit to water sources; discussion with camp management and sanitation staff	See Chapter 8 for simple protection measures. Much can be done by organising defecation and water collection and distribution better.
Is treatment necessary? If so, what form of treatment is needed? Can and should the water be disinfected (even if the source is not contaminated)?	Visits to water sources; water collectors; local water department	See Chapter 8 for simple emergency water-disinfection methods.

Table 2.1 Checklist for field assessment of water-supply and sanitation needs in emergencies (continued)

Questions	Sources of information	Comments
Water supplies (continued)		
Is the water at the source sufficient for short-term and long-term needs? Is the current water supply reliable? How long will it last at current and anticipated rates of use? Are water sources permanent or seasonal?	Visits to water sources; local water department; local people; hydrological and hydro-geological reports and records	Note possible seasonal variations in water availability, particularly for surface waters. Use a fixed depth gauge to assess changes in standing water volume.
Can the quantity of water available be increased, e.g. by developing a spring, or by improving access to a stream?	As above; also look at improvements made to nearby water sources if there are any	See Chapter 8 for simple methods to improve water availability. Note the possible impact on nearby water sources of increasing yield for the emergency settlement.
Is the water available to everyone, or is access restricted for some people?	Home visits; surveys at public places, e.g. distribution points	Reasons why water is not available to some people may be complex and may relate to exclusion from other basic rights, such as food and shelter. Seek local advice on this.
Is the water available only for the disaster-affected population, or is it used by local people too?	Water collectors; local people; officials; home visits	Conflict over water sources can be very serious. Consider the risk of spreading disease from the camp to the local population or vice versa.
Are there any alternative supplies nearby? How far, and how accessible? Are there any legal obstacles to using the alternative source?	Water authority staff; local government; local people; aerial photos, hydrogeological records; water source and route inspections	Note legal and financial implications, and involve the co-ordinating body as much as possible.
Is it possible to tanker water if local supplies are inadequate?	As above; local government roads department	Note seasonal variations in access, and logistics and financial implications if considering tankering.
Is it possible to move the settlement if water supplies are inadequate?	Local authorities; site visits; existing topographical, geological, hydrological, and natural-resources information on possible alternative sites	A decision needs to be taken early in the emergency if moving the settlement is considered.

Table 2.1 Checklist for field assessment of water-supply and sanitation needs in emergencies (continued)

Questions	Sources of information	Comments
Excreta disposal		
What is the current defecation practice? If it is open defecation, is there a designated area for this?	Site visit; discussion with sanitation staff	Close co-ordination needed here.
Are there any existing facilities? If so, are they used, are they sufficient, and are they operating successfully? Can they be extended or adapted?	Site inspection; population concerned; sanitation authorities in urban situations	Note water quantity needed to keep existing system running, and maintenance needs. Look at possible sharing arrangements to increase access to limited existing facilities if necessary.
Does the current defecation practice threaten to contaminate water supplies, food stores, or living areas?	Site inspection; site plans and maps	This is a site-planning issue: co-ordination between sectors is essential.
Are current defecation practices and facilities (including open defecation) a health threat to the users?	Inspection of facilities; discussions with users; health information	Very dirty toilets will not be used; evidence of this is usually to be found on the ground nearby.
What are people's current beliefs and preferred practices concerning excreta disposal?	Discussions with intended users; information on their previous situation and habits	Observed practice is far more reliable than answers to questions about preferences and practice.
Are people familiar with the construction and use of toilets? Are they prepared to use latrines, defecation fields, trenches, etc?	As above; site visit to see if people are building their own toilets independently	Don't make any assumptions on this question. A latrine programme designed on the assumption that people will build their own toilets will fail if the assumption was wrong.
Is there sufficient space for defecation fields, pit latrines, etc? What is the slope of the terrain? What is the level of the ground-water table? Are soil conditions suitable for on-site excreta disposal (permeability, diggability, and stability in particular)?	Site inspection; maps; hydrogeological and geological data; information from local people on seasonal variations in these parameters; percolation tests, trial pits, and soil-texture tests	These parameters are crucial to the technical feasibility of a latrine programme and they largely determine the technical options possible. They may add considerable weight to arguments for or against a particular site.

Table 2.1 Checklist for field assessment of water-supply and sanitation needs in emergencies (continued)

Questions	Sources of information	Comments
Excreta disposal (continued)		
Are sufficient local materials available for constructing toilets?	Local markets; forestry department; materials being used for shelter construction	Check the possible environmental and economic impact of the choice of local materials.
Do current excreta-disposal arrangements encourage disease vectors, particularly flies and mosquitoes?	Inspection of facilities; reports from members of the affected population; insect numbers	Try to predict and avoid vector breeding connected with excreta disposal. Counting insects is a time-consuming process and does not necessarily identify the breeding site.
Do people have access to water and soap for washing hands after defecation?	Discussions with people; structured observations; markets; distribution reports; water distribution points and water collection and storage facilities.	Water is the critical factor, soap less so.
Are there suitable materials available for anal cleansing (or water if appropriate)?	Discussions with people	This is a need that is often overlooked, but it is important for hygiene and for personal dignity.
Are there materials and facilities available to allow women to deal with menstruation hygienically and with dignity?	Discussions with women and girls; markets; distribution reports; observation of privacy available in shelters and toilets	As above.
Vector-borne disease		
Are there any vector-borne disease risks? If so, what are they, and how serious are they?	Health data on the disaster-affected population; local communities; information about previous exposure of the affected population to vector-borne disease	An assessment of risk factors and disease occurrence is often more practical than assessing the presence, type, and behaviour of disease vectors, which needs specialist competence.
If vector-borne disease risks are high, do people have access to individual protection (bed-nets, protected shelters, repellents, etc.)?	Household surveys; distribution records	Check that bed-nets are being used correctly. Check that access to these resources is available to all sections of the community and to all family members.

Table 2.1 Checklist for field assessment of water-supply and sanitation needs in emergencies (continued)

Questions	Sources of information	Comments
Vector-borne disease (continued)		
Is it possible to make changes to the local environment (by drainage, scrub clearance, excreta disposal, refuse disposal, etc.) to discourage vector breeding if necessary?	Inspection of breeding grounds; discussion with local people; measurement of water flows; hydrological and hydro-geological records and maps	It is very hard to assess the probable impact of environmental modification, particularly when several breeding sites exist in and around the settlement.
Is it necessary to control vectors by chemical means? What national programmes, regulations, and resources for vector control and use of chemicals need to be taken into account?	Vector-borne disease-risk factors and clinical data from health staff; Ministry of Health, WHO, and Ministry of Agriculture may have information on protocols and policies to follow	See Chapter 10.
Solid-waste disposal		
Is solid waste a health problem?	Site inspection; discussions with affected people; reports of rats and flies in particular	It is difficult to make a direct link between solid waste and health. The priority is to reduce vector-breeding sites, blockages of drainage channels, and sources of water contamination.
What type and quantity of solid waste is produced?	Site inspection; discussions with affected people; distribution records for food and other commodities; markets	It is possible to take representative samples of solid waste and weigh and measure them; but this is time-consuming, and these parameters are liable to change seasonally and depending on what is being distributed.
How do people dispose of their solid waste? Can solid waste be disposed of on site, or does it need to be collected and disposed of off site?	Site inspection; discussions with affected community and local government	See Chapter 11.
Are there medical facilities and activities producing waste? How is this being disposed of? Who is responsible for this?	Discussions with agencies concerned; inspection of health and related facilities; inspection of the settlement for medical waste	It is important to establish responsibility for disposing of medical waste. If possible, it should be disposed of inside medical-facility boundaries.

Table 2.1 Checklist for field assessment of water-supply and sanitation needs in emergencies (continued)

Questions	Sources of information	Comments
Drainage		
Is there a drainage problem (flooding shelters and latrines, vector-breeding sites, polluted water contaminating living areas or water supplies)? What seasonal variations are there? Where does the surface water originate?	Site inspection; discussions with people; vector-related disease information from health agency; discussions with local people; maps; hydrological and hydro-geological information	Try to establish early on to what extent any drainage problems are connected with the location of the settlement, for informing discussions on the longer-term choice of site, or arrangement of the site.
Do people have the means to protect their shelters and latrines from local flooding?	Discussions with people; tool distribution records	Consider how small-scale drainage works relate to major drainage routes. Check that people are willing and able to carry out small-scale drainage to protect their homes and toilets.
Hygiene promotion		
What facilities and resources for safe hygiene practice are available, and what needs to be improved?	Water-supply system and its operation; numbers and distribution of toilets; drainage, refuse-disposal, and vector-control programmes	Note whether access to these services and facilities is equitable, and whether or not any special efforts are needed to ensure that all sections of the community have access.
What are the key hygiene risks and behaviours for attention? • child/infant defecation • adult defecation • anal cleansing • cleaning children's bottoms • child stool evacuation • hand washing after anal cleansing • hand washing after cleaning children's bottoms • water collection • water storage • source of drinking water • management of domestic animals • breast-feeding practices	Site visits; household surveys; structured observation; key informants; focus-group discussions	Assessments should be simple and focus on a small number of risks and behaviours. They should relate to existing knowledge of the water supply and sanitation situation. Note any obstacles to improved hygiene practice.

Table 2.1 Checklist for field assessment of water-supply and sanitation needs in emergencies (continued)

Questions	Sources of information	Comments
Hygiene promotion (continued)		
What is the best composition of the hygiene-promotion team: gender, age, ethnic background, etc.?	The affected population; anthropological and sociological sources	It may be important to check this carefully before the assessment, to ensure that information on hygiene is collected sensitively and reliably.

2.3 Field assessment techniques

Field assessments for water supply and sanitation employ many techniques used in other fields, so the following comments apply specifically to water supply and sanitation but also to assessments in general. Below are some examples of field assessment techniques, presented in an order which reflects an increasing level of participation of the affected community. They range from techniques such as aerial observation and site inspection, which involve the community only as the subject of observation or counting, to techniques borrowed from Participatory Rural Appraisal (PRA) and Rapid Rural Appraisal (RRA), such as ranking and discussion, which involve the affected people as active participants in the assessment and analysis of problems and possible solutions. The degree to which different types of technique are appropriate depends on the sort of information required, the time available, and the extent to which it is considered necessary to involve people in analysis and decision making. It is generally appropriate to use less participatory and more rapid techniques for initial assessments to gather basic data on the size and nature of the emergency and to make estimates of the scale and type of response needed, if at all. But as soon as conditions allow, more participatory techniques should be used, to ensure that solutions considered are acceptable to and appropriate for the mix of people in the population concerned, and that they are suitable for the longer term.

As with any technique, the value of the information that these methods produce depends very much on the skill and organisation of the assessment team, and on the interpretation of the data.

2.3.1 Remote/ technical assessment

This includes surveys from the air, views from high points (hills, vehicle roofs, high buildings), and photographs taken from all these vantage points. These techniques may be enhanced by the use of existing satellite or aerial photograph images. This is a very rapid method to assess the scale of a disaster, to prospect for possible sites for emergency settlements, and to assess the movements of refugee and displaced populations.

2.3.2 On-site visual assessment

This can be combined with mapping and photography for documenting conditions and providing information for analysis and planning. See Chapter 6 for more detail on mapping techniques. An on-site visual assessment is usually done on foot or in a vehicle. This may be a structured and focused process, such as a health-observation walk or structured observation, in which a number of particular issues are observed during progress around the site, such as the number and location of water sources, their condition and intensity of use, and what parents do when their children defecate on the ground. (See Almedom *et al.* (1997) in 'Further reading' at the end of this chapter.) It may also include a sanitary survey to assess the likely risk of contamination of a water source and measures needed to reduce that risk. Either of these first two techniques may be used to estimate the number of people involved, either directly or by counting shelters or cooking fires.

2.3.3 Expert measurement and testing

Specialist knowledge and experience may be needed to carry out processes such as water sampling and analysis, inspection of sewers or pumps, or identifying disease vectors. This is commonly combined with advice from key informants and may be backed up by previous records.

2.3.4 Surveys

Surveys are used to gather statistically valid information from a representative sample of the population or from a sector of the population. They can provide rapid answers to questions about water consumption (including the variation in consumption between households and sections of a settlement); access to water containers; access to toilets; knowledge of hygiene, and attitudes and practice; and prevalence of diseases related to water and sanitation. This statistical information is a powerful tool for advocacy, planning, and measuring impact later on. Three stages are involved in a survey.

1. Establishing the survey technique

This involves establishing the population from which the sample is to be randomly selected (for example, the total population, the population in one part of the settlement, the population of mothers of children under 5 years old), and establishing the sampling method and number of individuals in the sample. The number in the sample is typically between 100 and 200 people, but the number chosen will depend on the degree of accuracy and reliability that is sought, the time and resources available, and the sampling technique chosen. The sample size does not depend on the size of the total population. There are several sampling techniques, suitable for different types of survey.

2. Carrying out the survey

This involves selecting individuals or households according to the sampling technique chosen, conducting interviews, measurements, or observations of the sample, and recording and collating information. This can be a major undertaking, involving training and mobilising significant numbers of staff. On the other hand, it could be relatively simple, for instance interviewing patients leaving a clinic to find out what disease they are suffering from, and what water-supply and sanitation problems they face.

3. Processing and interpreting the results

This involves processing the information recorded, using standard statistical techniques, depending on the survey technique chosen, in order to assign figures to the results. This information is typically presented in the form of a percentage or proportion, rather than absolute numbers. Also useful is a measure of the accuracy of the quoted figures. Often this is provided by a '95 per cent range'; roughly speaking, this gives a lower and an upper figure between which the real value is expected to lie, to a fair degree of probability.

2.3.5 Interviews

Interviews are used to collect detailed information about specific issues which cannot be gathered by simple observation. For instance, many practices connected with hygiene are not easy to observe, because they are carried out in private when possible. Interviews may be more or less structured, depending on the sort of information to be collected and how it is to be interpreted and presented. Interviews may be held with the following types of respondent.

- **Key informants:** to gather information rapidly on a particular topic, such as the location of wells, seasonal variations in surface water levels, or common practices regarding defecation. Both women and men should be included as key informants. There is always a risk that the information is unreliable because of the possible personal interests or perspective of the informant, and his or her information should be verified. Key informants are often people who speak the language of the field worker or who are easy to approach for other reasons, and they may be very unrepresentative of the general population.

- **Formal leaders:** to gather information about community structures and to encourage participation in programme implementation. Formal leaders may or may not be representative of the general population and may or may not have the population's interests at heart. Again, verification is necessary.

- **General groups:** to gather general information about how the disaster has affected people and what their intentions and ideas are.

- **Focus groups:** these are groups of people with a particular interest in the topic on which information is sought, or people whose views might otherwise not be noticed in the collection of information on a more general level. For instance, they may be a group of people collecting water, or a group of children, or a group of women at an ante-natal clinic, who may have particular needs or preoccupations.

- **Households and individuals:** to ask about access to water-supply and sanitation services, and resources and hygiene issues at the household and individual level. Household interviews may be used to gather detailed information with in-depth discussions, or they may be the basis of household surveys, where a large number of households are visited. Household visits are also an opportunity for visual inspection of toilets, water storage and use, and food hygiene.

Most of these techniques can be combined in one way or another. For instance, a visual assessment on-site is usually combined with key-informant interviews or focus-group discussions (for instance, talking with a local technician during the visual assessment and stopping along the way to talk with people collecting water). Many of the techniques are ones that field workers may already use informally. The purpose of giving names and structures to the techniques is to enable them to be used in a consistent and comparable way, and for results to be recorded and communicated clearly and effectively. It is important to ensure that techniques of designing, implementing, and interpreting surveys are sound, or there is a risk that unreliable information will be given false credibility, simply because it is presented in a quantified form.

2.3.6 PRA and RRA techniques

These are typically highly interactive techniques, which demand time and patience from assessors, but which allow people from the affected community to express their own opinions on their situation and contribute to analysis and decision making. For agencies with a commitment to working in a participatory way, these assessment techniques are a means to build this approach into the programme from the beginning. As with all assessment techniques based on information gathering from a sample of the population, care should be taken to ensure that a range of views is noted and that general conclusions are not drawn from an unrepresentative group of informants. These techniques are particularly useful for getting an understanding of how resources and activities are shared within the community, how different sections of the community are affected by the disaster, and what (in detail) is likely to be the impact of the proposed water-supply and sanitation activities. Some examples of PRA and RRA techniques are listed below.

- **Ranking**: participants are asked to rank various elements of their situation, such as the need for washing facilities, the need for taps closer to shelters, or the need for more water-storage vessels, symbolising their choices with long or short sticks, for instance. This can help field staff to understand people's perceived priorities and also give an opportunity for them to discuss programme options and possible constraints, and explain the agency's views.

- **Diagramming**: using maps, charts, or other visual means of portraying relationships in time (calendars of activities), space (maps and transects), resources (relationship diagrams), and others. These are very useful for collecting information — for instance on the location of local water sources, seasonal variations in disease incidence, or availability of labour — and for gaining an understanding of how people in the affected community view their situation. It can also be used as a means of understanding how the agency itself is perceived.

- **Discussing**: the various forms of discussion described above can be used as part of a participatory assessment, and are a good way to cover general issues and find out what to explore in more detail.

2.4 Interpreting and presenting assessment information

2.4.1 Interpretation

Information from different sources should be cross-checked; detailed information should be used to validate general information; and general information should be used to extrapolate detailed findings.

As in all forms of investigation, it saves time and focuses attention to have an idea of the information needed and the way it will be used before field work starts. Each area of water supply and sanitation requires answers to specific questions for decision making, and the checklist in section 2.1 can be used to ensure that all important areas have been covered. It is useful to make a list of specific assessment questions on a piece of paper while doing the assessment, so that information can be quickly filled in and important issues are not forgotten. Not all information gathered is needed in a report. For instance, records of stream flow for water-source assessment will not usually be presented, but it is useful to keep such records, in case data have to be verified later on. No standard reporting format is suggested here, but an appropriate report format can be designed, using the assessment checklist.

It is important to make a judgement on whether or not the situation demands external assistance and, if so, what that assistance should be. The judgement should take into account local capacities and the actual or proposed activities of other agencies. Some assessment of these two factors is necessary for the judgement to be made.

An assessment of priorities is also important, to enable plans and strategies to be formulated, and to ensure that the most urgent needs are addressed first.

Additional background information on the local area, the people involved in or affected by the disaster, and likely outcomes helps decision makers, who may be remote from the emergency situation, to understand the context.

An assessment of logistics needs, possibilities, and constraints is a specialised field, and in a large emergency there should normally be logistics specialists involved in the assessment. Logistics questions to be addressed include transport routes, handling and storage facilities, local supplies, and security for goods. See Chapter 5.

2.4.2 Assessment report

An assessment report should include some or all of the following sections, many of which are common to reports in all sectors. In some situations the water and sanitation report may form part of a multi-sectoral assessment report. If an agency has a standard reporting format, then this should be used.

- Title, author(s), agency, location and date. Important for identifying the report and tracing the source of information, because many situations generate several reports.
- Executive summary with key recommendations, proposals, budget outline and resource implications. Important to allow busy people to find the main points quickly.
- Background to the emergency and key features that have implications for programme-related issues.
- Methodology and timing of assessment.
- Key results, including population figures (broken down by age and sex), key problems to be addressed related to water, sanitation, and hygiene (health data and notes on access to adequate water supplies and sanitation); other agencies' activities and plans.
- Description of water and sanitation facilities, including current state of repair, operation, and use.
- Detailed recommendations. Not necessarily a project proposal, but at least a list of actions recommended, with priorities and timing.
- Resource implications (human, financial, logistical, etc.).
- Terms of reference (if they have been specified).
- Appendices: relevant analyses of data, maps, design drawings, etc.

2.5 Assessment strategy

Emergency situations change rapidly, and it takes time to develop a full understanding of the contextual and technical issues involved. It is very rarely possible to carry out an initial assessment that produces all the information necessary to design and implement an emergency response. An appropriate strategy is to aim for a very rapid initial assessment, within a matter of hours or days, in order to appraise the scale and nature of the emergency and priorities for action, if any is needed. This should be sufficient to get an initial response started, and needs only approximate information on population figures, access to resources, major disease problems, and existing capacities. At an early opportunity, within a few more days, this initial assessment should be refined and updated, in order to produce a more substantial and detailed understanding and plan of action. This process of reassessment may need to be repeated several times as the situation develops and needs change. The programme may be reviewed occasionally throughout its life, using many of the same assessment questions and techniques. Assessment, monitoring, review, and evaluation are related processes which feed into each other and do not have strict boundaries.

Tips for field assessments

- Use all the senses. Water-supply and sanitation problems can usually be seen, touched, smelled, tasted, and heard about.
- Get several opinions on the situation from different points of view. Ask the same questions in different ways. In complex situations, try to get beneath the obvious responses.
- Consult men, women, children, old people, disabled people, and representatives of all ethnic groups in the affected community.
- Be aware of whom you represent. This will greatly influence the quality of information you are likely to receive.
- Try to get figures. Reliable quantitative data are essential for describing the problem, for assessing its severity and the measures to take, and for establishing baseline information for monitoring and evaluation.
- Be aware of the limitations of the data you may collect and the extent of their inaccuracy or reliability.
- The assessment is only as good as the reporting of it. The report from a field assessment has to present the information needed to persuade other people that there really is an emergency, to start programme design, to set objectives, to write budgets, and to present proposals to donors.
- Good communications systems are vital to ensure that reports and information are delivered to decision makers fast, and to keep people up to date as the situation changes. Ensure that you can feed back the results of the assessment quickly, to allow speedy and informed decision making within your organisation.
- Use up-to-date maps. Make them, if necessary.
- Make, use, and record up-to-date lists of key contacts whom you need to meet.
- Always carry a pen and paper to record meetings, observations, data, and ideas.

- Try to get an overview before going into the detail on site.
- Talk to people and explain what you are doing and the possibilities *and constraints* of a possible response by your agency.
- Share your findings with others.
- Collect only the information that you think you will need. Don't waste time on unnecessary surveys. Concentrate on priority areas.
- Present your findings with arguments to show how you reached your conclusions. You may not be present to provide the details at meetings where programme decisions are taken.

Further reading

A. Almedom, U. Blumenthal and L. Manderson (1997) *Hygiene Evaluation Procedures: Approaches and methods for assessing water- and sanitation-related hygiene practices,* Boston: International Nutrition Foundation for Developing Countries (INFCD)

J. Davis and R. Lambert (1995) *Engineering in Emergencies,* London: RedR/IT Publications

J. Good (1996) 'Needs and Resources Assessment', Topic 3 of *New Approaches to New Realities: First International Emergency Settlement Conference,* University of Wisconsin — Disaster Management Center, Madison, USA

S.J. House and R.A. Reed (1997) *Emergency Water Sources: Guidelines for selection and treatment,* Loughborough: Water Engineering and Development Centre (WEDC)

MSF (1997) *Refugee Health: An approach to emergency situations,* London and Basingstoke: Médecins sans Frontières/Macmillan

P. Perrin (1996) *War and Public Health: Handbook on war and public health,* Geneva: ICRC

N.S. Scrimshaw and G.R. Gleason (eds) (1992) *Rapid Assessment Procedures: Qualitative methodologies for planning and evaluation of health related programmes,* Boston: International Nutrition Foundation for Developing Countries (INFDC)

Sphere Project (forthcoming, 1999) *Humanitarian Charter and Minimum Standards in Disaster Response,* Chapter 2, section 1, 'Analysis', published in Geneva by the Steering Committee for Humanitarian Response (SCHR) and Interaction; e-mail: sphere@ifrc.org; internet: *www.sphereproject.org*

M. Thomson (1995) *Disease Prevention through Vector Control: guidelines for relief organisations,* Oxford: Oxfam

3 | Planning and implementation

3.1 Project plans, budgets, and proposals

In order to start an emergency response, it is necessary to follow a logical process of defining the problem, setting objectives for a response, listing the means needed to meet those objectives, and then securing funds to acquire those means. This need not take a long time, and agencies with substantial resources of their own may be able to commit themselves to a project on the basis of a rapid initial assessment, knowing that they will find time to refine their understanding and analysis as the situation unfolds, and that they can secure funding later on if necessary. There are several elements to the process of translating assessments into water-supply and sanitation projects.

3.1.1 Analysis

On the basis of the information gathered during the assessment, an agency has to decide whether or not to get involved and, if so, what to do. This means balancing a number of immediate and strategic concerns, some of which relate to the particular agency's own policies and capacity, and some of which relate to broader issues.

3.1.2 Objective setting

All projects should have objectives. Even in the most urgent emergency, any agency that intervenes should have stated aims, more clearly defined than 'saving lives'. Setting objectives need not take a long time, and they may be very simple, such *as 'provide 5 litres of potable water per person per day within one week for an affected population of 20,000 people'*, within an overall aim to *'reduce diarrhoeal mortality and morbidity due to water-related disease to normal regional levels within two months'*. Without objectives, a project has no justification and no direction, and it cannot be judged to be effective or not. Objectives should be SMART:

Specific: specifying the conditions that the project aims to change;

Measurable: in quantitative and/or qualitative terms;

Achievable: given the constraints and opportunities of the situation;

Relevant: relevant to the problems identified in the assessment;

Time-bound: the timeframe for achieving the objective should be specified.

Objectives should be set for the project as a whole, and for each of its major components, and for the managers responsible. These different levels of objectives should relate to each other in a direct sequence of cause and effect. The most useful levels of objectives for emergency water-supply and sanitation project planning are **outcome objectives**, or changes within the affected population, such as use of toilets or hygiene behaviour or water consumption, that can be related directly to the programme; and **output objectives**, which are the results expected in terms of goods and services provided, such as numbers of tap-stands or latrines constructed. Higher-level objectives, or **goals**, such as reducing the incidence of diarrhoea or improving health, are difficult to relate directly to any one intervention or even to a group of water and sanitation interventions, and are less useful as programme-management tools, though it is clear that water supply and sanitation contribute greatly to improvements at this level.

Objectives may be established with the participation of the affected community, if there is the time available. Some of the RRA/PRA techniques mentioned in Chapter 2 can be used for doing this, as well as for identifying objectives within the project team.

3.1.3 Project plans

The project plan should specify the objectives and activities of the project, identify what inputs are needed, and include a budget. **Indicators** for monitoring and evaluation defined at this stage will help to keep the project on course and ensure that activities remain relevant to original objectives. An indicator is a significant variable (for example, litres of water per person per day, or number of people per toilet), used to measure change. See section 4.1 for more on indicators. Plans should specify the timing of the planned activities and achievement of objectives. Planning frameworks such as the logical framework are a useful way to organise information, define project components, and clarify relationships between activities, the results they are designed to achieve, and the resources needed to carry them out. The terminology used for the different levels in this framework will be used throughout the book. The word **'objective'** is taken to have a general meaning, denoting a state or a change that a project is designed to achieve; it might apply equally to goals and outcomes (sometimes known as 'wider objectives' and 'immediate objectives'). Specific terms will be used in this book for describing levels of objective. This terminology can vary, according to agency or donor, but presenting a hierarchy of project objectives in a framework, such as the logical framework outlined in Table 3.1, is increasingly required by major donors, and is a useful planning tool in any case.

Table 3.1 Outline logical framework for project and programme planning

Narrative summary	Objectively verifiable indicators	Means of verification	Assumptions
Goal: what is the wider objective, or the problem that the project will help to solve? *e.g.: control morbidity and mortality*	What are the quantitative ways of measuring, or qualitative ways of judging, whether these wider objectives have been achieved? *e.g. Crude mortality rate, malaria incidence*	What sources of information exist or can be provided cost-effectively and time-effectively? *e.g. Records kept by health centres, community health workers, and graveyards*	
Outcomes: what are the intended immediate effects on the project target group? What are the intended benefits, and to whom will they go? What improvements or changes will the project bring? *e.g.: adequate access to clean water supply and toilets, and the means and information to practise good hygiene*	What are the quantitative measures or qualitative evidence, by which achievement and distribution of effects and benefits will be judged? *e.g.: access to toilets (people per toilet, distance to toilets); water-consumption figures (litres per person per day; percentage of people washing hands before eating)*	What sources of information exist or can be provided cost-effectively and time-effectively? Does provision for information collection need to be made under Inputs? *e.g.: household water-use survey; structured observation; records of use of public latrines*	What assumptions are made about achieving outcomes leading to a contribution to the Goal? *e.g.: it is assumed that progress is made in other sectors*
Output: What outputs (kind, quantity, and schedule) are to be produced by the project in order to achieve its planned Outcomes? *e.g.: number of latrines built; litres of water distributed; number of households visited by hygiene-promotion workers; number of houses treated by vector-control spraying team*	What are sources of information? *e.g.: record books of community-based sanitation workers; water-system logbooks; water-point surveys; team-leader records*	What assumptions are made about producing outputs leading to achieving outcomes? *e.g.: it is assumed that all households have access to the water points installed*

Table 3.1 Outline logical framework for project and programme planning (continued)

Narrative summary	Objectively verifiable indicators	Means of verification	Assumptions
Activities: *e.g.: assessment and planning; latrine demonstration; materials distribution; water-system design, construction, and maintenance* .... **Inputs:** *e.g.: staff, materials, equipment, vehicles* .... **Budget**		What are sources of information? *Activity reports; construction logs; stores and materials records; vehicle logs; financial records*	What assumptions are made about activities, inputs, and budget-producing outputs? *e.g.: it is assumed that the design of water system is technically feasible, given the conditions encountered*

Each sector of the project may have its own outcomes, outputs, and activities, but their relationship should be made clear in the planning framework. Plans may be divided into several stages, each with its own objectives, according to different phases of the work. For instance, the first-stage objective may be to set up a water treatment and distribution system to provide 5 lcd (litres per caput [head] per day) of potable water within 1 km of each shelter for a population of 20,000 people within one week; and the second-stage objective may be to increase the quantity supplied to 10 lcd and develop the distribution system to bring water to within 500 metres of each shelter within one month.

Once project plans have been drawn up, the project can be broken into its various components and an activity plan produced. This identifies the key activities to be undertaken, who is responsible for their completion, and how long they are expected to take. This information can be displayed as a planning chart, which is simple for project staff and other colleagues to read. The purposes of a planning chart are to help to ensure that all necessary activities are planned for and resourced; to identify activities that may create critical delays and which may need particular attention, or additional resources, or alternative strategies; and to help to monitor progress.

More sophisticated time-planning tools, such as critical path analysis and others which are frequently used in the construction industry, may be applicable in some circumstances. However these are generally more useful for linear processes which can be planned with a moderate degree of certainty than for projects which react to quickly changing needs and operating environments. The value of project plans depends on the quality of information on which they are based, and there is often a danger that plans do not reflect the reality of the situation or the real needs to be addressed. It should be constantly borne in mind that the purpose of project planning, as with any other project-management tool, including assessment, monitoring, and evaluation, is to enable projects to be established and managed so as to address problems effectively and efficiently. Unless it achieves this, it is not worth spending time on it.

3.1.4 Budgets

Emergency budgets are rarely more than good estimates of likely costs, made in uncertain situations with incomplete knowledge. But a well-written budget, based on good information and analysis, makes a valuable contribution to the smooth running of a project, quite apart from the fact that it is required by potential donors. Budgets should be detailed enough to allow financial monitoring of different project activities, but flexible enough to allow the project to adapt to new conditions or new information. The information upon which budgets are based should be the inputs listed in the project plan. It is very useful to have the costs of major items to hand in the field, to put together an accurate budget rapidly. Different agencies and donors use a variety of budget structures, and it may be necessary to divide spending categories in a particular way, according to specific requirements for financial planning and reporting.

3.1.5 Project proposals

Proposals to donors should be concise, with a short summary, background information, analysis of the situation, justification for assistance, objectives and strategies for action, important assumptions, activities planned, timetable, and budget. It is important to know each donor's requirements and procedures for financial reporting and transferring funds. A number of different formats are required for project proposals by different organisations and donors, but most proposals should contain the following sections. Much of the information can be summarised in a logical framework.

- Summary
- Background
- Goals, outcomes, and strategy for proposed project
- Assumptions (important to allow you to argue for changes in the plan, if necessary)
- Activities planned
- Phase-out strategy
- Resources needed
- Budget

3.2 Phased response

The following is a guide to conditions and actions for environmental health during different phases of a refugee situation.

Phase 1: Days or weeks — acute emergency

Conditions: Families and individuals may undertake exhausting journeys or undergo a period of danger, suffering and stress, and may be malnourished, ill, traumatised, and disoriented. Community structures are often weak: families may be broken up and children lost. Conditions may be crowded, with inadequate shelter, water supply, sanitation, and food. The risk of epidemics of diseases such as cholera, malaria, and measles is high. There may be a rapid increase of other background diseases and poorly operating health services, and mortality rates may be very high (2+ deaths per 10,000 people per day). There may be a lot of political and military instability and uncertainty about the future of the settlement.

Aims: Protect life and health with rapid and possibly short-term assistance, until more permanent solutions can be found, such as relocating people or setting up adequate water-supply and sanitation systems. The breathing space provided should be used to gain a clearer understanding of the situation and the possible future of the settlement; to consult with the affected population; to plan a longer-term intervention; and to raise funds, recruit staff, order and receive equipment, etc. for putting in place longer-term measures if appropriate.

Actions: Identify priority needs and ensure response capacity. Recruit and establish a project team capable of implementing an immediate response. Obtain reliable (if approximate) population figures and health information, if possible disaggregated by age and sex. Start to identify key individuals in the community, to ensure rapid implementation of first measures. Identify and protect key water sources to avoid contamination and aim to provide at least 5 litres per person per day. Designate areas for defecation. Assess for, plan, and start implementing actions for the longer term as soon as possible. **Do not delay. Do what is possible straight away and concentrate on priorities.**

At this stage, the six most crucial aims are the following:

- to provide facilities for people to excrete safely and hygienically;
- to protect water supplies from contamination;
- to provide enough water for drinking, cooking, and essential personal and domestic hygiene;
- to ensure that people have enough water containers to collect and store water cleanly;
- to ensure that people have the knowledge and understanding they need to avoid disease;
- to ensure that people have soap for washing their hands.

Phase 2: Weeks or months — stabilised emergency

Conditions: Families and individuals start to settle in, and community structures are reassembled or new ones formed. If first-phase public-health measures have been effective, then morbidity and mortality rates will be under control and falling.

Aims: Ensure that minimum standards for water supply and sanitation are met, and contribute to bringing key morbidity figures down to background rates, and bringing crude mortality rate down to less than 1 death per 10,000 people per day, or to the background rate. Establish positive conditions for longer-term programmes, including resettlement or return if appropriate.

Actions: Develop health-information system (see section 4.1.2) and contacts with community for information gathering, hygiene education, and promotion of programme. Start implementing longer-term technical solutions. Set up water abstraction and treatment works with limited distribution system for extending later on. Start building family-type latrines shared by several families, or public latrine blocks preferably of a design that can be handed over to families later on. Monitor vector-related disease statistics and react where necessary.

Phase 3: Months or years – post-emergency

Conditions: Families and individuals are established in the settlement, with longer-term social structures and activities established. Morbidity and mortality remain at or near the levels in the surrounding areas or the area of origin.

Aims: Reduce dependence on outside assistance, increase local capacity, and help preparation for return, resettlement, or rebuilding.

Actions: Consolidate health-information gathering; review health information monthly and as special situations occur. Complete water-distribution systems and increase water supply to at least 15 lcd. Consolidate operating procedures and training of staff for possible eventual handover. Ensure that permanent washing facilities, family latrines, drainage systems, etc. are in place and that systems for maintenance and cleaning are sustainable. Monitor vector-related disease statistics and react where necessary.

3.3 Planning horizons

Some emergencies are over in just a few weeks, and the people affected are able to resume their normal lives again without need for further support. Many others, however, continue in one form or another far beyond the immediate stages where urgent action is required. Refugees may remain in camps for many years, dependent to a large extent on outside aid. After an earthquake it may take months or years to repair damaged water supplies and clear up debris.

Short-term actions should be taken with an awareness of the longer-term context; otherwise unnecessary long-term costs may be incurred, such as systems that are expensive to run, people who are more dependent than necessary on outside aid, reliance on large numbers of international staff, and damage to the local economy and environment. For instance, an excreta-disposal project which begins with strong measures to force people to use defecation fields, withholding ration cards from families until they build their latrines, might achieve good short-term results, but creates a difficult relationship between refugees and sanitation workers and may make a more collaborative approach very difficult in the future. The importance of looking ahead when making technical choices is illustrated by the Mozambican refugee camps in Malawi, where local timber was used for latrine-slab construction for several years. Some slabs had to be replaced three or four times because of termite damage. This was very costly in terms of local deforestation and a large annual sanitation budget. After some years the timber slabs were replaced with concrete ones, which were used until the refugees left.

3.4 Co-ordination and integration

3.4.1 Options for co-ordination and integration

In Chapter 1 the importance of co-ordinating and integrating the various components of water supply and sanitation projects was mentioned. There are several ways in which this can be done; the most suitable way depends on the scale and complexity of the problem, the capacities of the different agencies present (including their available funds), the number of agencies present, and the policies of co-ordinating bodies.

In many ways, integration of different activities within the same agency is the most effective and efficient system, as plans, information, and resources are more easily shared, particularly if there is flexibility in the allocation of funds to the different parts of the project or programme. For the affected people themselves, it is arguably easier to deal with a single agency working on water, sanitation, and hygiene promotion than with three or more different agencies with different ways of working and different contacts within the community. Co-ordination of funding between implementing agencies, co-ordinating bodies, and funding agencies also helps to ensure that all important sectors are supported.

On the other hand, large emergencies pose problems of water supply and sanitation that a single agency cannot solve, and some division of responsibility is needed. In this case, effective inter-agency co-ordination is essential. This requires not only a strong co-ordinating body but also agencies which are interested in related areas of water supply and sanitation beyond their specific responsibility, and willing to share information and adapt their projects according to need. There is always a danger of gaps in service provision or awareness of problems. For instance, the need to avoid drainage problems at water points may be overlooked by both the water-supply agency and the sanitation agency. A problem of scabies in one part of the camp may be identified by the health agency, but the water-supply agency may not be aware of it and so fails to address a possible problem in the distribution system. The activities of one agency may even be damaging to those of another, as in the example of unco-ordinated siting of wells and latrines. If staff responsible for the various aspects of the project are able to bear in mind that they are primarily involved in health-related work and have some notions of public health, this sort of problem is less likely to arise.

Integration has another sense, one that implies outside agencies integrating their activities with those of local government and NGOs. Most emergencies result in the establishment of parallel systems for health, water supply, and sanitation. This is usually necessary at first, because local capacity is inadequate to cope with the situation and it is impossible to increase this capacity in the time required. But if they are well managed, external agencies can be encouraged and obliged to integrate their activities with national programmes and local initiatives, and in so doing leave something of lasting benefit, such as trained government staff, locally appropriate water supplies, or improved techniques for excreta disposal.

Co-ordination and integration are, perhaps, most important in the early stages of an emergency response, because the situation changes daily, and priorities have to be adapted to changing needs. The links between water supply and excreta disposal are particularly crucial when conditions are bad and the risk of contamination of water supplies are so great. Daily co-ordination meetings are often needed within and between agencies to ensure that priorities are addressed, gaps are not left, duplication is avoided, and resources are shared. As situations become more settled and projects are established, weekly or monthly sectoral co-ordination meetings should be sufficient, in addition to specific meetings to address urgent problems that may arise.

It is important to involve representatives of the affected community in the co-ordination process, as a means of ensuring that activities are approved by them and in order to inform the affected community of the agencies' plans and to encourage participation and co-operation.

3.4.2 Co-ordinating water supply, sanitation, and hygiene promotion in practice

- Integration and teamwork are the responsibility of all team members and must be supported by all levels of management.
- It is vital that all those involved are helped to understand what hygiene promotion is and how it can contribute to the programme and project outcomes.

- It is important that one person co-ordinates the hygiene-promotion aspect of the programme; this person can be either an engineer or a health promoter.
- Assessments should be seen as a joint activity to provide crucial information for project planning and design; for example, the identification of water sources and priority sources to be protected.
- Meetings with community members that involve discussions regarding the design of facilities should initially be attended by both engineers and hygiene promoters.
- Planning the project should be a joint activity, and initial objectives should be discussed and defined together.
- It may be helpful to write joint reports regarding work progress; but if this is not possible, then team members should at least read and discuss each other's reports.
- Regular meetings between team members must be held.
- Visits to other team members' project sites will help to promote integration.
- Hygiene-promotion workers can also be involved, when time permits, in such activities as water testing or visits to other projects or engineering sites.

3.5 Contingency planning and preparedness

3.5.1 Introduction

The speed with which first-phase emergencies can be brought under control and with which sickness and death can be reduced depends very much on the preparedness of the organisations concerned, and also on the ability of the affected community to react and organise in the face of an emergency. Accepting that there is often little that is done or can be done to deal with the processes and events that give rise to population displacement or infrastructure damage, it is possible to gather information which allows some advance planning to be done. Then, when a disaster does occur, some preparation has already been made, in terms of securing stocks of equipment, identifying staff, and making links with other agencies and government departments so that the response is co-ordinated. By strengthening the capacity of local communities and institutions through disaster preparedness and mitigation, it may be possible to avoid emergencies or reduce their impact. This important area of work is outside the scope of this book, but should not be ignored, particularly by those agencies which have the means and the breadth of experience to work on capacity building as well as emergency response.

3.5.2 Contingency plans

Experience has shown that events are very rarely predictable, and that it is usually a waste of time and effort to make detailed contingency plans and arrangements for emergencies. It may be possible and useful to do detailed planning for a specific event such as a volcanic eruption, but conflict and the population movements generated by the event are hard to anticipate with any certainty. Nevertheless, it is useful to be aware of crises that may develop, to make and update an inventory of local response capacity to meet various possible problems, and to assess one's organisation's own resources and capacities at field and central levels, in case they are needed. These resources may include trained staff or access to new staff with specialist skills; equipment, either locally or centrally held; funds and fund-raising opportunities; transport and storage facilities; and local contacts and knowledge. In general, the more centrally held the contingency capacity is, the more flexibility there is in its geographical application. On the other hand, an agency's local capacity may be more informed and responsive.

3.5.3 Training

Training of staff in emergency assessment and programme implementation speeds up and improves the quality of the response. Practical workshops, visits to established emergency programmes, and staff exchanges help to increase knowledge and build confidence. Training staff already employed on established programmes builds their ability to assess and react to new emergencies. It may be possible to train individuals on the basis of specific responsibilities assigned in anticipation of an event. For example, pump operators or water-treatment technicians may be trained to set up and run emergency water systems, as teams with specific roles and management lines identified. Training may be provided on all aspects of the emergency response, including gender analysis and participatory approaches.

3.5.4 Pre-prepared equipment and techniques

Knowing that for large populations the most likely water source will be surface water (to ensure the quantities needed), it may be possible to put together a package of water-supply equipment to meet immediate needs and to start installation of a more permanent system, with the very minimum of information about available water sources.

3.5.5 Local contingency stocks

In areas that are likely to receive refugees, contingency stocks of suitable equipment can be kept locally. These stocks should provide all the equipment needed to allow the staff available at short notice to start implementation during the time it takes for more equipment to arrive. Contingency stocks need careful management to avoid their being used up on non-emergency work, and to protect them over time from the weather, rodents, etc. The aim should be to stock a small amount of equipment to allow a response to be started while more equipment is brought in. If additional stocks can be delivered fast, there is no point in storing more equipment than can be used by the staff immediately available. Local delivery by land can take longer and be far more complicated than air transport from a central base, particularly if the equipment has to go from one country to another one.

3.5.6 Sites

In planning for a possible arrival of refugees, it may be useful to identify sites to settle them. Knowledge of the sites means that designs for water-supply and sanitation systems will be more thorough and can be implemented more quickly, and it should be possible to avoid choosing unsuitable sites in the rush of refugees arriving. It may sometimes be possible to prepare basic infrastructure on sites before the arrival of people, such as the camps prepared in Jordan for people fleeing from Kuwait in 1990.

3.5.7 Access and logistics

A vital element of contingency planning is to research the possible ways of reaching the emergency site with staff and equipment. Contacts with transporters and suppliers allow the agency to assess different options and allow transporters and suppliers to make their own plans to meet the agency's possible needs.

3.5.8 Contingency plans for established systems

Even in the most stable refugee situation, conditions may change quickly There may be security problems preventing access to the camp with supplies of fuel for pumps, or an unexpected drop in the water-table, or a strike of workers. There may be a new influx of refugees or an outbreak of cholera. These things should be anticipated and planned for as far as possible, with sources of equipment and additional staff identified in case they are needed. Training and planning can save time when dealing with foreseeable problems such as seasonal outbreaks of cholera, or drying up of wells. Where security may be an issue, camp-based staff should have the resources and authority they need to manage activities for some days, in case access to the camp is impossible. The more responsibility that is given to locally based staff, the less chance there is of collapse when outside help is cut off. Some technical measures can be taken with water supply and sanitation systems to make them more reliable in times of crisis. See Chapter 8 for more detail of contingency planning for established water-supply systems.

3.6 Operation and maintenance

Specific recommendations on operation and maintenance (O&M) are mentioned in the sections on individual aspects of water supply and sanitation, but below are a few general points to bear in mind. They apply primarily to water supplies, but are equally relevant to other areas involving centrally managed services, such as public latrines maintenance or refuse collection.

- Operation and maintenance of systems start as soon as they go into operation and may be needed for several years.
- O&M needs to be planned, budgeted for, and managed just as carefully as construction does.
- Monitoring of system performance, consumption of fuel, chemicals, and spare parts, staffing, spending, major repairs, and replacement of equipment is an essential part of operation and maintenance. Systems for monitoring need to be established from the beginning of the project.
- O&M needs constant attention, to ensure that standards of supply do not slip and that systems do not gradually fall into disrepair. Monitoring system performance is a part of this.
- The work and cost involved in O&M is affected by the way the systems are designed and built in the first place. Construction work is often done at a time when money is readily available, and this opportunity should be used to build systems that will be cheap to run when money is more difficult to find later on.
- Core staff involved in system construction are best placed to run the system. Keep a small team of plumbers, masons, and others for repairs.
- Involve the service users as much as possible, to reduce the work involved in O&M, for instance by organising water committees to look after tapstand areas and washing facilities and to carry out simple repairs.
- As-built systems designs, original plans, and operations manuals are vital tools for understanding how the system works and for tracing and solving problems. System plans should be updated as modifications are made.
- Spare-parts catalogues for mechanical equipment are essential for the correct specification when ordering spare parts.

Family latrines and other household-based or community-based services may need quite a different approach, and this is discussed in the relevant chapters.

3.7 Handover

It is often difficult to plan, at the beginning of an emergency intervention, the optimum duration of the project and at what stage to withdraw; but agencies planning a quick intervention and early departure should start to identify an exit strategy early on. If the involvement of an outside agency in the emergency response is seen as a response to a lack of local capacity in the face of a disaster, then in principle agencies should transfer control to a local organisation — governmental or non-governmental – that will be responsible in the longer term. This may involve finding another organisation to take over the work, or giving the responsibility to the affected people themselves. Successful handover to another agency requires a good analysis of that agency's capacity to carry on the programme to the desired standard — the quality of its staff, its track record for similar work, its access to funds. and its own long-term plans — and a considerable period of joint planning, training, and monitoring. Oxfam GB handed over water systems in some of the Rwandan refugee camps of Bukavu, Zaire in late 1994, but was obliged to return to the camps soon afterwards to carry out remedial work and training over some months, because the handover process and departure from the camps had been too rapid. Attention to the following points should make handover more successful.

- *Handing over takes time.* Unless the local agency or government department has a lot of experience in running water-supply systems, the process can take several months.
- *Handing over involves extra activity.* This includes additional training, revision or writing of plans and manuals, discussions, and meetings. This needs planning, budgeting, and managing.
- *Handing over should be a staged process* which allows the level of support to the local agency to be revised if necessary. It may be appropriate to keep some longer-term low-level contact with the project if the agency taking over needs advice or information that may have been overlooked in the handover.
- *The ability of the agency taking over to finance and manage the work should be considered.* Its access to supplies, cash, and technical support should be appraised. Its ability to continue operations in case of difficult circumstances should also be considered.
- *Good records are essential* to help the new agency to keep projects running as planned. Important documents include site and system plans, staff lists, and descriptions of operational and monitoring procedures.

The more responsibility that is devolved to site staff and users, the less there will be to hand over, if site staff remain with the project.

3.8 Closing down emergency settlements

Eventually many emergency settlements are abandoned, as their inhabitants go home or are resettled. There are a number of options for using water-supply and sanitation installations, as follows.

- *Leave installations in place* and adapt them, if necessary, for use by local people who may move to the settlement, or for use in possible future emergencies. It may be necessary to make significant modifications if the expected population is much smaller, and make the installations suitable for more local operation and maintenance as part of a national system.

- *Recover equipment for use elsewhere.* This may be in a nearby local settlement, or another emergency settlement. Again, the suitability of the equipment for the alternative use has to be confirmed, and support given if necessary for establishing and sustaining local operation and maintenance. Care should be taken to ensure that correct dismantling and transport is carried out, to avoid losing or damaging vital pieces of equipment.
- *Recover equipment and store it for possible future disasters.* This demands very careful attention to correct dismantling, packing, labelling, and storing the equipment; otherwise it may be of very little use when it is needed. Mechanical equipment may need extensive service or repair, and many components may need replacing in order to make up complete kits. It may be more expensive to recover and re-pack equipment than it is to purchase new items.

There may be a temptation to carry out projects simply because equipment is available when a site is abandoned. This should be avoided. If projects are worthwhile and equipment can be recovered for their implementation, this is good; but that should not be the reason for adopting them.

Ownership is another important issue to address when planning what to do with equipment from abandoned emergency settlements. It may be that the equipment legally belongs to the host government, under the terms of the project agreement. It may belong to the funding agency or the implementing agency. Or it may belong in a legal or other sense to the national government, or to owners or traditional users of the land that the settlement occupied.

If it is expected that equipment can be adapted, or recovered and reused after the emergency, this may influence the choice of equipment. For instance, this may be a good reason to purchase pumping equipment locally, rather than to import the agency's standard stock.

Another important consideration when sites are abandoned is their rehabilitation and possible future use for agriculture or resettlement. It may be necessary to back-fill latrines, make safe medical-refuse disposal facilities, and dismantle potentially dangerous structures. This may require considerable resources and it needs to be planned.

Closure of an emergency settlement can involve significant costs, and these need to be adequately budgeted.

Further reading

J. Davis and R. Lambert (1996) *Engineering in Emergencies: A practical guide for relief workers* (Chapter 4), London: RedR/IT Publications

L. Gosling and M. Edwards (1995) *Toolkits: A practical guide to assessment, monitoring, review and evaluation. Development manual 5,* London: Save the Children

4 | Monitoring, evaluation, and reporting

Much of this section refers to ideas and terms used in the logical framework in section 3.1.3.

4.1 Monitoring

4.1.1 Why monitor water-supply and sanitation projects?

The purpose of monitoring is to provide management information to ensure that the project is going according to plan, that it responds to and meets high-priority needs, and that resources are being used efficiently, effectively, and equitably. **Effectiveness** is a measure of results achieved. **Efficiency** is a measure of results achieved in relation to resources used. Information produced during monitoring may also be useful for sharing with the affected population and other agencies, and for programme evaluations.

In the field of public health, monitoring is also known as the **surveillance operation** or **health information system (HIS) operation**. This provides the global public-health monitoring framework for the various sectors involved in the humanitarian response.

4.1.2 What to monitor

There are many different aspects of projects which can be monitored, and which may be appropriate to monitor in certain circumstances or for specific purposes. However, monitoring systems should be kept as simple as possible for ensuring adequate management information without becoming a management burden. For managing and measuring most water-supply and sanitation programmes, four major project aspects are usually monitored. These relate to four key questions that managers need to ask:

1   Does the project respond to public-health needs (does it contribute to goals)?
2   Is the project having a positive impact (are desired outcomes being achieved)?
3   Is the project going according to plan (are planned outputs being produced)?
4   Are resources being used efficiently (are inputs producing the activities and outputs planned)?

1. Public-health and related information: GOAL level of logical framework
This includes background information on diseases related to water supply and sanitation, population figures, population movements, and other major issues related to the project. Health and population figures should be used to inform project decisions. For instance, an increase in diarrhoea incidence in one part of the settlement should be investigated, and action should be taken to strengthen activities there. This link between health information and project activities is particularly important when dealing with epidemics, and it is important that information flows fast between the HIS and the water-supply and sanitation sector. Normally the water-supply and sanitation staff would feed information into the HIS, which is managed by health staff in a co-ordinating role. Information fed to the HIS would include (as a bare minimum) rates of water consumption, access to water points, and access to toilets. Information received from the HIS by the water-supply and sanitation staff might include general and location-specific water-related and sanitation-related disease figures and epidemic information.

Sources of information: Regular health reports using data from health centres, outreach activities, and feeding centres; deaths recorded; occasional survey data relating to health and nutrition; census and registration records, population-movement reports, food and non-food distribution records.

2. Project impact: OUTCOME level of logical framework
This is a measure of the impact on the disaster-affected people that can be directly attributed to the project. It can be a difficult indicator to measure, as it involves assessing not only the project output (number of tap-stands, number of toilets, etc.), but what difference those outputs have made to people's lives. Examples include monitoring the amount of water *consumed* (as distinct from the amount of water *produced*), and the number of people *using* toilets (as distinct from the number of toilets *built*). Measuring these indicators may involve surveys or other forms of information-gathering in the affected community, and is usually more costly and time-consuming than measuring output (see below). It may be done occasionally to verify that the project outputs are actually achieving positive outcomes in terms of access to improved water supplies and sanitation.

Sources of information: Surveys of (for example) water use or amount of refuse in the settlement; reports from the affected community; disease figures, particularly diarrhoea incidence and malaria incidence, where applicable, from health staff.

3. Project progress: OUTPUT level of logical framework

It is useful to divide this category of indicator into two types, one for construction or project development, and one for operation and maintenance or on-going activities.

Construction/project development: For instance, how many latrines have been built? How many people have had access to hygiene education by health visitors? This demands record-keeping by field staff such as storekeepers, construction team leaders, community-based water and sanitation staff, health workers and others.

O & M/on-going activities: Once systems are running, they need monitoring to ensure that they are performing correctly. This applies to systems for water treatment, pumping, latrine emptying, latrine replacement, vector-control activities, refuse collection, vehicle use, etc. Records should be kept on standard sheets, filled in by system operatives or supervisors.

Sources of information: Construction progress reports; record sheets for system operation (water production, hygiene education sessions, refuse collection, etc.); regular surveys, e.g. of latrines actually in use, for outputs that may need eventual replacement or repair.

4. Project resources: activities and inputs level of the logical framework

Activities are needed to achieve outputs, and usually require inputs (staff time, materials, equipment, and money). It is usually sufficient to monitor inputs and compare these with achievements (outputs). For instance, on a pipe-laying job it is common to monitor staff hours spent per distance of pipe laid (input per output), but not to monitor the specific activities of the pipe-laying team, which are something of an operational detail, best left to the team to organise. Very often outputs and resources are monitored and recorded on the same reporting sheet. For instance, a water-treatment technician will record on one sheet the amount of water treated, the amount of chlorine used, and the residual free chlorine level measured in the treated water. In this way, if there are discrepancies between these indicators, they can be checked and action taken straight away.

Managers may also want to monitor aspects such as safety, environmental impact, and equipment and material stocks. In fact many of these are routinely checked, although staff may not regard this as a monitoring activity.

Sources of information: Monthly spending reports; staff timesheets; vehicle logbooks; stock records; purchase records, etc. Although most of these sources of information should exist as part of normal project activities, some information, particularly on project output, may require surveys or other additional information-gathering exercises.

4.1.3 Setting up a monitoring system

Bearing in mind the four questions above concerning relevance, results, progress, and resources, managers should set up an appropriately simple monitoring system from the beginning of the project, because it becomes very difficult to do so later on, and important information gets lost. The number of indicators used should be the minimum necessary to enable effective project management. When choosing indicators, first decide what management information is needed; then choose indicators that are:

- **Reliable and objective:** indicators may use quantitative or qualitative information, but this information must be based on fact rather than impression, supported by evidence if needed, and possible to verify by use of the same measurement method.

- **Relevant** to the aspect of the project to be measured. For instance, a spraying team's report on its activities is more relevant than a storekeeper's report on insecticide used, as an indicator of the number of houses sprayed. But the indicators should tally.

- **Timely:** the indicator should produce information that is available sufficiently fast to allow decisions to be taken in time to correct problems or adjust to new circumstances. Thus deaths from diarrhoea are a serious indicator of water and sanitation problems, but information on a fall in water availability in one part of the settlement indicates the problem more rapidly and allows corrective action to be taken in time to prevent deaths.

- **Sensitive** enough to allow an understanding of project and context to a relevant level of detail. So while it is not necessary for a manager to know the location of every toilet in the settlement, it is important to know if there are areas where access is poor and where special attention is needed.

- **Based on available data** as far as possible. Avoid having to set up additional information-gathering systems and activities, and duplicating monitoring activities. Monitoring should use information that is routinely available and part of programme implementation. This information may be collected by other agencies or colleagues working on other projects, such as health. In some situations, community workers or leaders may be collecting information routinely.

- **Simple** enough to use information that can be collected by staff with minimal training, which remains reliable, even in unfavourable conditions, and is straightforward enough to be understood by non-specialists.

Once the indicators are chosen, you should decide how often to monitor them. This will depend on how fast the situation is changing, and the degree to which each indicator is critical to important decisions. So, for instance, figures on diarrhoea incidence and water consumption may be collected daily at a time when the water-supply system is being developed rapidly and there is an outbreak of diarrhoea. At another time when the situation is more stable, weekly checks are sufficient. The information on water production and diarrhoea incidence will continue to be recorded daily by water-treatment and health-centre staff as part of their routine activities, but will not be monitored so frequently when it is no longer necessary.

Monitoring is made much easier if data-recording systems are set up in a standardised way, so that staff simply have to fill in boxes on record sheets to note their routine activities and anything else worth noting. Examples include pump operators' log books recording pumping hours, fuel and oil consumption, volume of water pumped, and repairs and mechanical problems; or a spraying team's log book noting the number of shelters sprayed, the dosage rate, the application rate, the amount of chemical used, etc. All of this detailed information may be strictly irrelevant to everyone except for the water-treatment or spraying-team leaders, but when summarised it provides a regular picture of the programme which can form part of the monitoring system. Monitoring of specific activities is discussed in the relevant technical chapters.

Once reporting forms are produced, staff need training in their use, and occasional spot-checks to ensure that they are recording information correctly. It is important that they understand the value of the exercise, which may seem like a waste of time, and also that they do not simply provide the information that managers are expecting or would like to see.

4.1.4 Managing the monitoring system

- Collect record sheets from project staff and other relevant sectors (health, administration, shelter, etc.).
- Verify, using spot-checks or cross-checking with other sources of information where necessary.
- Collate and summarise information relating to key indicators chosen.
- Analyse: look for trends and events in the data, check progress against plans, look at links between inputs, activities, outputs, and outcomes (if measured).
- Report, share, display, and feed information back to project staff, the affected population, and other sectoral staff (particularly health staff), as appropriate.
- File reports so they can be retrieved and used for comparison and future reference.
- Consolidate reports.

4.1.5 Reporting

Much of the monitoring system produces information that is of interest only to the project team, or to parts of the team for internal decision making only. For instance, reports from the logistics team on materials taken for the latrine programme may be compared with reports from the sanitation team on latrines constructed every two weeks.

External reports are also needed for use by the programme team and others, including other staff of the same agency or staff of other agencies, and the affected population. It is common to produce external reports every week, two weeks, or month, depending on the situation and the project. These may be consolidated to produce quarterly, six-monthly, annual, or end of project/end of phase reports. These consolidated reports should present the major achievements, trends, and events of the period and tell the story of the project during that time. In addition, donors may have their own particular reporting requirements, which are useful to know early on, so that the relevant information can be collected as a routine activity.

4.2 Evaluation and review

4.2.1 Purpose

Projects are evaluated to see whether they achieved their objectives (for instance, whether minimum standards were achieved, and how quickly they were achieved), whether they did this in an efficient and effective way and, sometimes, what other effects the project had. The results of an evaluation should be used for learning and improving work. Evaluations need not wait until the end of a project: the most useful evaluations are often done in time to identify important things to change in the project. This type of evaluation is often called a **review**, or **interim evaluation**.

The information collected during an evaluation depends on the questions asked. These may be restricted to the original aims of the project, using indicators chosen at the planning stage; or they may look much more widely, for instance, to assess the economic or environmental impact of the project, which may not have been considered at all at the outset, but which may be of great importance.

The costs of evaluation should be allowed for in the project budget, to ensure that funds are available, and to make staff aware that it will be one of the planned project activities.

4.2.2 What to evaluate

The three principal questions usually asked about a project are listed below.

Was it effective? In other words, did it achieve what was necessary to meet the needs of the affected population? Were the objectives the right ones to achieve the overall goal? Were the project assumptions correct?

Was it efficient? Did it achieve this in a way that made efficient use of resources?

Was it equitable? Did it meet the needs of all parts of the community?

Answers are sought by evaluating the achievement of several levels of objective, principally the following:

- *Outcome:* Was the desired impact achieved? This may be direct impact, such as improved access to water and sanitation; or indirect impact, such as an improvement in morbidity and mortality figures. The contribution of the water-supply and sanitation programme to improvements achieved by a combination of actions in a number of areas, including health services and nutrition, may be estimated.
- *Outputs:* Was the planned number of taps installed? Was the planned number of sanitation volunteers trained? If not, then why not?
- *Inputs:* Was the budget all spent? Was it overspent? If so, why?

It is useful to look at the links between the different levels of objective, in order to measure efficiency. For instance, the outcome objective of a hygiene-promotion project was to increase the percentage of people washing their hands after defecating from 20 per cent to 80 per cent. (This implies that baseline data were collected to establish the rate of handwashing after defecation at the start of the project.) The actual increase achieved over the project period was only 40 per cent, even though all the inputs were used as planned. The reasons for this low impact may be found to be internal to the project (inaccurate assessment, poor management, corruption, activities not carried out as reported, etc.), or to be connected with the technical assumptions on which the project was designed and implemented (for example, that soap would be available). So the lessons to be learned may be specific to the project being evaluated, or relevant to other projects.

Process indicators, which are less directly related to the impact on the affected population, but are of great importance to the ability of the organisation to operate effectively and efficiently, are also commonly evaluated. They include information about logistics, personnel and administrative procedures and performance, decision making and management, and security procedures. Evaluating these aspects of the project may be important for understanding the success or otherwise of the water and sanitation element and for judging the organisation's ability to perform adequately in other situations.

In addition, it may be necessary to examine some of the effects of the project that may not have been included in its objectives, such as environmental impact, impact on the local economy, access to services for local people, the impact on the workload and status of women, or the impact of the project on social organisation within the affected community. Evaluating these issues is easier if the need is anticipated early on and information relating to the pre-emergency situation is gathered. It may be that one agency takes responsibility for investigating one or several of these issues.

4.2.3 Sources of information for an evaluation

The sources of information used will depend on the questions to be asked and the resources available. Sources include the following:

- **Assessment information:** this includes the background information gathered as part of the assessment process, as well as the assessment report itself. It is useful for establishing a clear picture of the situation before the emergency response started and for understanding why project objectives were set.

- **Monitoring information:** monitoring reports provides a record of project implementation and important developments in the situation, and helps us to understand how the project developed through its life. Information in these reports can be condensed to provide a short summary of the project, listing original objectives, achievements, and costs.

- **Other programme reports:** these include internal and external reports which may be concerned with specific issues, such as security, or an outbreak of malaria, or floods in part of the emergency settlement. These reports give a picture of some of the major influences on the programme and events which explain certain decisions or changes. This also includes reports from related sectors such as health and management.

- **Field information:** it may be necessary to gather fresh information to fill gaps in reports, measure indicators which were not measured as part of the monitoring process (commonly indicators of outcome or impact, which may be difficult to measure routinely), or learn specific lessons as part of a wider operational research process. Field information may be gathered by talking with staff at all levels, and by using the full range of field assessment techniques mentioned in Chapter 2. These include surveys and participatory techniques, important for understanding how people from the affected community perceive the project and for gaining a detailed understanding of its impact at the individual and household levels. Reference to the original assessment or assessments can enable a 'before and after' picture to be created.

4.2.4 Project review

The most useful evaluations are often those carried out part-way through a project, designed to examine progress, test some of the assumptions on which the project is based, and suggest improvements for its future. In many emergency situations it is possible to take time, relatively early, to stand back a little and reconsider ways of working, objectives, and strategies. Assessment and review largely overlap in the early stages of an emergency, and are part of the same cyclical process. It is most important that projects adapt as situations change, so that the first-phase type of approach is not continued into later phases, with resulting problems such as chronic overwork, short-term planning, lack of attention to administrative detail, and lack of consultation with the affected population. Conversely, projects which have been established for some time and which have lost their emergency features may benefit from a review to ensure that a capacity to react to new problems is maintained and that the project is moving in the direction planned, and not stagnating. It may be useful to have external assistance with this process, for instance from a professional facilitator, or staff from headquarters or another agency.

4.2.5 Using evaluation information

All too often, evaluation reports are filed and forgotten, either because they raise questions that people find difficult, or because they are not considered to be relevant to the project or the organisation. This is a waste of money and time. The use of the evaluation information should be clearly considered before planning the evaluation itself, and a commitment should be made to acting on its findings. The ways in which the information is to be shared should be considered before writing the report, so that it can be done in a way that all the intended readers can understand. This may also require translation, illustration, and a presentation programme to share the report widely.

The information may be shared in part or in whole with the following people, among others:

- programme staff, to allow them to verify or challenge it, to learn from it and to add to it if necessary;
- the affected community, to allow them to judge its accuracy and relevance and to suggest further improvements, if appropriate;
- staff from other implementing agencies, to help them to understand the programme and lessons for their own work;
- co-ordinating, funding, and host-government agencies, to report on the programme, and demonstrate the agency's achievements and openness to scrutiny;
- fund raisers, to communicate with the giving public about what has been, or can be, achieved with their support;
- support staff within the agency, such as technical support or administrative support teams, to help them to understand projects and improve institutional knowledge and support activities, including training;
- researchers and trainers, to help lessons leaned to be incorporated into the broader body of knowledge and improved practice concerning emergency situations.

Further reading

B. Broughton and J. Hampshire (1997) *Bridging the Gap: A guide to monitoring and evaluating development projects*, Canberra: Australian Council for Overseas Aid (ACFOA)

J. Davis and R. Lambert (1996) *Engineering in Emergencies: A practical guide for relief workers*, Chapters 4,7,8, and 9, London: RedR/IT Publications

L. Gosling and M. Edwards (1994) *Toolkits on Assessment, Monitoring, Review and Evaluation*, London: SCF (UK)

MSF (1997) *Refugee Health: An approach to emergency situations*, London: Médecins sans Frontières/ Macmillan

Sphere Project (1999, forthcoming) *Humanitarian Charter and Minimum Standards in Disaster Response*, Chapter 2, Section 1, published in Geneva by the Steering Committee for Humanitarian Response (SCHR) and Interaction; e-mail: sphere@ifrc.org; internet: *www.sphereproject.org*

5 | Managing project resources

Once an assessment has been done, an intervention agreed, and a plan, however preliminary, has been drawn up, resources have to be assembled and managed rapidly for project implementation to start. This chapter deals with the resources that are the direct responsibility of managers and technical staff. It is assumed that funding for the project is obtained, but that field managers are responsible for monitoring its spending.

5.1 Materials and equipment

Most water-supply and sanitation interventions depend on the use of materials and equipment. Even helping to organise separate locations for defecation and living areas involves some material support. The speed and quality of engineering interventions will depend to a great extent on the quality and design of the materials and equipment used, and it is most important that all stages of its management, from specification to installation, are well managed.

5.1.1 Type of equipment

The assessment will determine the type of materials and equipment needed. These are the key questions to be answered: how many people have to be served? How rapidly does the equipment need to be installed? Are there special considerations, such as acceptability, technical challenges, and local technical capacity that demand a certain type of system or resource to be distributed? Urban situations demand a very different technical approach from cases of displacement into rural areas, and possibly quite different materials and equipment. Rapid-response equipment may be appropriate in some situations, but not in others.

There is a wide range of emergency water-supply and sanitation equipment now available on the market, and its provision has become a very big industry in recent years. Some relief agencies have their own preferred equipment which is suitable for their ways of working, the staff they employ, and the technical support they can provide to field workers. Much of the equipment is standard to the water industry, but has been adapted and combined with technology for agriculture and food handling. Equipment should have the following features, among others:

- It should be readily available in the right quantities, and straightforward to pack, store, and transport.
- It should be relatively simple to understand and explain, and easy to assemble in the field under difficult conditions, and with staff who may not be familiar with it.
- Information must be provided on assembly, commissioning, and operation; and on maintenance, where relevant.
- It needs to be robust and hard wearing.
- Adaptability is important: can it be put together in a variety of ways to meet different needs?
- It should be simple to operate and tolerant of abuse.
- Spare parts should be easily obtained, and maintenance should be straightforward.
- It should be easy to fit with other equipment used by other agencies.

Oxfam GB first used standardised water and sanitation packs in the early 1980s and has an on-going programme to improve the specifications of equipment used and to explore new techniques and equipment as they become available. The equipment range includes water pumping, storage, treatment and testing, and ground-water development equipment, as well as other equipment for sanitation and shelter.

5.1.2 Rapid-reaction equipment

Lightweight, rapid-reaction water equipment has been used for several years by a number of agencies for acute emergencies. This includes bladder tanks (pillow tanks), flexible pipework, lightweight pumps, and tap-stands. This equipment is easy to transport, quick and simple to use, and may be installed, used, packed up, and moved elsewhere easily if the population moves on. It allows the possibility of a rapid response without a large capital investment in one particular site, and helps to provide minimum water supplies before more permanent and higher-capacity supplies can be installed. Lightweight excreta-disposal equipment is less well developed, although some emergency excreta-disposal techniques such as defecation zones do not involve any heavy equipment, and many other techniques rely on local materials. It is often possible to carry some lightweight water equipment on assessments, which could be used to set up a simple pumping, chlorination, and distribution system.

5.1.3 Specification

Exact specification is important, to ensure that the correct purchases are made and that the materials and equipment used on site perform as intended. Wrongly specified supplies, such as generators which are not powerful enough for the pumps they are intended to run, or an incorrect formulation of insecticide, are costly and cause delays and hardship in the field. Standard specifications, which might apply to emergency stocks or to goods held by suppliers or manufacturers, can help to save time and ensure that equipment is robust, complete, simple to install, compatible, and good value for money. Many organisations, including Oxfam, have detailed specifications for a large range of emergency equipment. The UNDP Inter-Agency Procurement Services Office (IAPSO) produces technical specifications for items for emergency relief in consultation with a number of agencies.

In many circumstances specification may be needed for particular applications, for instance replacing specific components of an urban water-supply system, or choosing the correct insecticide for controlling a particular species of mosquito in a particular environment. In such cases it is essential to seek advice from someone who is competent in the specialist field.

5.1.4 Emergency stocks

Materials and equipment may be standard or non-standard, and may be procured from two essentially different sources: emergency stocks and supplies purchased as and when needed.

Oxfam GB's experience over many years is that using emergency stocks of water-supply and sanitation equipment makes an essential contribution to its capacity to respond to emergencies. The advantages of holding emergency stocks include the following:

Speed: Supplies can be loaded and dispatched within hours of a request, and stocks can be managed to ensure a predictable capacity to respond.

Reliability: Materials and equipment stocked have been field-tested and are known to perform adequately.

Familiarity: Field staff may be familiar with the materials and equipment from having used them on previous projects, from being trained in their use, or because they are standard to the water-supply and sanitation professions.

Cost: Although there are considerable costs involved in tying up money in stock and in holding stock, savings can be made on bulk purchase, by avoiding purchase under pressure, and by being assured that the correct supplies are available. Yearly contract prices may also be negotiated.

Completeness: Holding stock enables materials and equipment to be assembled in the form of kits or modules, so ensuring that related and essential components are considered together when ordering and dispatching. Ordering from stock is relatively straightforward.

Tailored goods: It is possible to develop materials and equipment in collaboration with suppliers, as a long-term working relationship is created.

The disadvantages of using central stocks of pre-specified supplies include the fact that the equipment stocked may not be appropriate to needs in the field (this is particularly true of urban environments), and therefore may not be used or may be used in an inappropriate way; it does cost money to invest in stock and to manage it; and it can discourage local purchase and the development of local solutions.

5.1.5 Direct procurement

Some materials and equipment are not kept in emergency stores, because (like local building materials, or insecticides) they are too bulky, perishable, or difficult to stock and transport, or because they are too specialised to be of general use. Many agencies do not hold stocks, but purchase what they need when they need it as a matter of policy. The advantages of this arrangement include low overhead costs: the organisation does not have to tie up its own funds in equipment which may not be used for some time. Many of the advantages of holding emergency stocks are lost, however.

A compromise arrangement is to identify companies that can supply equipment and materials to standard specifications in anticipation of need. To be effective, this solution may require close consultation with the suppliers concerned, and visits to verify specifications, quality, stocks, and production capacity.

Local purchasing
In principle, local purchasing should be favoured over international purchasing, if it stimulates the local economy and offers better value for money. Local purchase may offer the advantage of compatibility with local practice and existing equipment; nearby availability of spare parts and replacement supplies; and local familiarity.

However, local purchases often go through merchants who do not necessarily keep their profits in the area or the country. The quality and availability of locally available goods may not be satisfactory. Local purchasing demands skilled and experienced buyers who can find goods that meet the specifications required at an acceptable price. Particular care must be taken to ensure quality control, including testing samples before purchase.

International purchasing
Many agencies choose to buy goods from their home country, because although it is often more expensive, there is often greater control of quality and specification. International air transport is expensive, but it is often faster and more reliable than local or regional road transport, particularly when international borders have to be crossed.

Regional purchasing

This can often be a good compromise, enabling regional buyers to purchase good-quality material at reasonable prices, within a few days' drive from the area where it might be needed. For instance, Nairobi in Kenya has been used by many agencies to buy goods for projects in the Horn of Africa and Central and East Africa. Buyers have to be particularly careful when purchasing goods like cement, pumps, and pipe that the specifications, design, and quality are up to standard. Pumps which break down and cannot be repaired because there are no spare parts available cost a lot more than their purchase price in terms of problems for field operations.

When deciding on an appropriate source of supply, it is important to balance the requirements of time, quality, specification, and cost. This balance should be reassessed regularly, because availability, cost, and transport opportunities change.

5.1.6 Transport

Managers in the field should not have to be too concerned with international logistics, which should generally be managed by logistics staff. Their responsibility is to ensure that goods needed from outside the project area arrive on time, in good condition, and within budget.

Air transport

Air transport is increasingly used for emergency logistics, particularly with the increasing involvement of military personnel. However, air transport is very expensive, and many goods can be transported by slower and cheaper means if their use and re-supply are carefully programmed. Goods transported by air are subject to safety restrictions, and materials like chlorine or aluminium sulphate may need special packing and permits before they can be transported by air. Make sure that there are unloading facilities and/or labourers on arrival to deal with heavy and bulky equipment. Make sure that paperwork is all in order and that responsibility for handling and clearing goods on arrival is clearly understood, as airport and customs authorities may hold planes and goods at the airport for days or weeks if all is not in order. Paperwork should arrive one to two weeks before the shipment if possible, to allow time for the customs process.

Surface transport

This is much cheaper than air transport, but is slower and in some situations is very unreliable because of bad roads, insecurity, or theft. Goods should always be carried with a written contract, which gives the transporter the responsibility for ensuring that all the goods arrive in good condition at their destination. Payment should be made conditional on a signed receipt by the receiving storekeeper to confirm the goods' arrival, noting any losses or damage.

5.1.7 Field logistics systems

In order to manage materials and equipment, a supply-chain management system is required, to ensure that a record is kept of their ordering, arrival, storage, transport, final use, and payment. Goods may be transported and stored several times before final use, for instance in a large programme with a central store and a store at each of several sites. An example is the Oxfam field stock-control system, which includes the following records, maintained at each level in the system.

- **'Supplies request' form** for ordering goods for the programme or for specific project activities, from a supplier, a central emergency stock (head office), or a field store. Correct use of the form ensures that only authorised requests are passed on to logistics staff; that all requests are formally recorded and dealt with in a systematic way; and that staff responsible for monitoring stock levels and project budgets can do so in a timely way.

- **'Goods received' form** for logging receipt of goods into the warehouse. It forms a record of all supplies arriving at the stores (goods may be checked and logged in and out without unloading at the store if they are to go directly to a field site in an emergency); it is used as proof of receipt for suppliers who may require formal acknowledgement of delivery; and it is used as a record when supplies delivered are incomplete, damaged, or incorrect.

- **Waybill** for recording the despatch of goods from stores, for stock management, to monitor goods in transit, and to monitor the speed and efficiency of the logistics system. It enables the dispatcher, transporter, and receiver all to know and agree on what is being carried between one place and another; it acts as a tool for monitoring stock levels; it acts as a check against theft or loss during transport; and it acts as a document for any authorities checking the load, and protects the agency from liability for any additional goods which are not listed.

- **Bin card** for recording each type of item held in stock, and to record every in-and-out movement of stock with cross-reference to the appropriate 'goods received' and waybill forms. Where the same type of item is needed for several projects or sites within the same programme, a card may be kept for each site or project, so that use and availability for each one can be monitored more easily.

- **Stock report** for presenting a summary of all stock movements into and out of a store during a set period, and an up-to-date record of theoretical stock balances (inventory). It is used as the basis for completing the stock reconciliation form.

- **Inventory form** is used to check that the information on the bin cards and stock-report form is accurate and that the logistics system is functioning as it should. It is a record of a physical count of the contents of the store, which should be carried out at least monthly.

This may seem to be an unduly complex and detailed set of forms to be used in an emergency. However, it is vital to ensure that goods which are purchased with limited budgets, transported often at the expense of other goods and at great cost, and which have the potential to make a significant impact on the health and lives of the affected population are not lost, stolen, or damaged. It is also essential for monitoring stocks of equipment and providing information in advance for reordering. The field stock-control kit is an essential tool for ensuring and demonstrating accountability to donors also.

5.1.8 Establishing and running a field logistics system

Setting up the system requires a great investment of time and energy. For a programme of any size, this is best done by dedicated logistics staff. They need to recruit and train a logistics team, set up procedures, and arrange warehousing, transport, and local purchase opportunities. Logistics staff may have many other duties, such as arranging staff and office accommodation, communications, and security. It is essential that water-supply and sanitation project staff make the job of establishing and running the field logistics system as easy as possible by following a few simple rules. Even if this occasionally means that individual requests take longer to deal with, the general result is greater speed and efficiency.

- Involve logistics staff in programme planning and decision making, and over-estimate needs rather than under-estimate them at the planning stage.
- Plan ahead to allow plenty of time for the logistics system to deliver in the most efficient way, rather than presenting last-minute or out-of-hours requests for urgent items, if this can be avoided. Maintain adequate stocks to enable work to continue while goods are en route.
- A regular stock-issue system (daily, weekly, fortnightly, or monthly) is more efficient than a system of irregular stock issue which cannot be planned for.
- Record the use of goods taken from stores, goods used, goods transferred between sites, and goods returned, lost and damaged, and transferred from one budget to another.

Linking goods used with progress achieved
It is very useful for field managers to relate goods used at a particular site or project with project implementation, in order to reduce the risk of loss or theft and to spot necessary changes in quantities of materials needed. Further goods for that site or project can be issued after a satisfactory report on the use of the goods issued for the previous period and the receipt of work-plans for the following period. This process may follow a very rapid cycle when activity is very intense, but may fall back to a longer cycle when activity is slower or more predictable.

Storing equipment
If at all possible, all water-supply, sanitation, and shelter equipment should be stored indoors. However, space may be limited, and much of the equipment used can be stored outside in most climates, as long as it is covered over and is within a secure fence or is well guarded. This applies to boxed equipment and pipes in particular, although it is good practice to cover these up to protect them from the worst of the weather and dust. Cement, tools, and loose fittings should be stored inside, and bins, shelves, or other means of keeping loose fittings separate and clearly identified should be used. Each fitting needs to be clearly named in the language used by field staff, to avoid confusion. This may require training and drawings, or a board with an example of each fitting and the accepted name underneath each one in a prominent place. Staff should avoid opening boxes to remove components, as this is inevitably forgotten and the equipment is dispatched to a site and found to be lacking a vital part. Equipment stores should be managed by carefully selected and managed warehouse staff.

Some materials and equipment inevitably have to be stored at the construction or operation site. This can have the advantages of autonomy for the site team in case of problems of access to the site; reduction in the number of deliveries needed; and reduced risk, if there are security problems near the central store. Any situation in which materials and equipment are stored in one way or another should be managed as part of the field logistics system, and the same concerns about correct storage apply.

Local buffer stocks and contingency stocks
It may be wise to keep a buffer stock over and above the minimum stock level for certain items, in case supplies are delayed or needs suddenly increase. The level of buffer stock should be agreed with the staff concerned and reviewed regularly. It is a waste to finish a programme with large stocks of materials and equipment not used, and these goods have to be accounted for. The size of buffer stock will also be influenced by storage capacity and budget.

Contingency stocks may be held for specific purposes. They may be marked and physically set aside, or simply identified in the stock records and the minimum re-order level set accordingly. Where perishable goods are set aside, they should be turned over regularly, and all contingency stocks should be regularly checked to ensure that they are not damaged and that they still function correctly. Managing contingency stocks needs considerable expenditure on warehouse rental, staff, security, and insurance.

5.2 Field staff

5.2.1 Introduction

The success of emergency water-supply and sanitation programmes depends on the quality, motivation, and support of staff at all levels in the implementing agency. A range of skills is needed in the field, from engineering to hygiene promotion and from project management to plumbing. Projects usually include people who work full-time for the agency, contract staff, both national and international, and refugee workers.

5.2.2 Field staff needs

The number and type of staff needed have to be determined on the basis of the project elements and, particularly in the case of construction activities, the speed of implementation necessary. It is important that management structures are put in place and operated well, so that staff are effective. This is often the most difficult task for managers in emergencies. Many different management structures are possible and appropriate for different types of situation and project, but the following guidance may be useful when deciding on a structure and on staffing needs.

1   *Identify the major project components and support departments to be managed and create a management team.* For example:
    - Emergency Programme Manager, who may report to a Country Programme Manager
    - Water Supply Project Manager
    - Hygiene Promotion Project Manager
    - Logistics Manager
    - Administration Manager.

2. *Identify activity-related teams for carrying out the field work.* The size and number of teams will be determined by the size of the tasks and the speed at which they are to be carried out. Each team should consist of no more than about 20 people, with its own team leader. For instance:
    - pipe-laying teams
    - tank-erection teams
    - chlorination teams
    - pumping teams
    - hygiene-promotion teams (usually divided up by areas of the settlement)
    - local logistics team.

3   *Choose intermediate management posts as necessary,* to ensure that field-based activity teams are as closely managed as needed and that the core management team is not over burdened. Intermediate management posts may be both geographically split (for example, one manager per camp in a

programme covering several refugee camps), and split by programme activity (for example, a Water Project Manager and a Hygiene Promotion Project Manager per camp, each reporting to his or her counterpart in the programme management team).

If a logical framework has been used for project planning, it can help to identify staff needs and the levels of management responsibility required.

5.2.3 Staff from the affected community

In most emergencies involving refugees and displaced people, it is they who do most of the work of implementing emergency projects, as engineers and technicians, administrators, community workers, health educators, craftspeople, and labourers. Some points to bear in mind when recruiting and managing staff from the affected community are the following:

Demands on time: Particularly during the early days and weeks of an emergency, the disaster-affected people may be traumatised, sick, disorientated, and preoccupied with the struggle to survive. They may not have the time or energy or motivation to work on water-supply and sanitation projects, unless they are adequately paid. Women in particular may be fully occupied with household activities at the early stages of an emergency, but might be brought into employment at a later stage.

Status and sense of purpose: On the other hand, many people affected by emergencies suddenly lose status and a useful role because of the crisis; for them, the chance to have a useful occupation, practise skills and learn new ones, take on some management responsibility, and maybe earn something can be a great opportunity.

Previous responsibilities: In many crises, for instance the case of Kurdish refugees in Turkey and Iran in 1991, or Rwandan refugees in Goma in 1994, a complete cross-section of society is involved, and engineers, doctors, lawyers, and teachers find themselves in the same camp with plumbers and peasant farmers. The range of skills and knowledge available may be greater than can be found in the surrounding area.

Local politics: One should be aware of the politics within settlements in emergencies, and the pressures that may affect staff, or the political influence that their position may give them. This may reflect on the perception of your agency and the project.

Payment: Staff from the affected community may work as unpaid volunteers; they may receive some form of material non-cash incentive; or they may be paid a regular cash wage. The arrangement chosen may depend on the local situation, and no solution is universally applicable. Some practical issues to consider are the following:

- *Poverty and needs:* People from the disaster-affected community may be extremely poor and in need of money or goods to help to support their families. The contribution of earnings from employment on emergency projects can be very important.
- *Management:* If very little or no payment is made, there is little chance of controlling the quality of work done, the hours worked, and theft of materials.
- *Local rates:* Payment rates should take into account national and local rates, rates paid by other relief agencies, rates in the area where people have come from, and the assistance that people might be getting in the form of food, shelter, and medical care.

These issues should be discussed with local authorities and other agencies, to establish a fair and cost-effective policy.

Social diversity

Agencies may choose recruitment practices which aim to give particular opportunities to women, men, old people, young people, disabled people, or others. The condition of women can be significantly influenced by their employment on a water-supply and sanitation programme which gives them a chance to earn money, be involved in programme decision making, or work in the community. The following points should be considered when deciding on a policy for gender balance in the recruitment of staff from the disaster-affected community.

Qualities: Who are the most suitable people for the posts to be filled? Consider technical skills, language skills, status and influence. Can men really do this job better than women, or is it something that both could do well?

Workload: Can people manage the extra work demanded, and what impact will their employment have on household-management activities?

Training: Check what training may be needed to ensure that both women and men have access to employment opportunities.

Contracts: Check national law regarding contracts, particularly for refugees, who may not have the right to be employed officially. In this case, a contract cannot be given. This has consequences for investment in staff, particularly training, though refugee staff may still receive incentive payments and value the opportunity to receive training.

5.2.4 Managing labour-intensive construction work

Management options

There are various options for managing large labour forces on construction activities, including the following:

Daywork: Staff are paid on a daily basis, regardless of work achieved. This may be important for skilled tasks, where quality is important as well as speed. It also gives managers a lot of flexibility in the way they deploy staff, allowing them to change tasks quickly in response to problems or changing priorities.

Piecework: Staff are paid for achieving certain tasks, which are agreed with the manager. This is suitable for tasks such as trench digging and pipe laying, where it is easy to define the quality of work needed and to inspect work to ensure that it meets quality standards, at the same time as giving the workers a strong incentive to work fast.

Task work: This is a combination of the above. A task is agreed for each day, and staff can leave when they have finished the day's task. This enables managers to plan and monitor progress on the basis of daily achievements, but can consume a great deal of time in daily negotiations.

Work should not be started until payment rates and other conditions have been agreed and understood by all concerned. Records should be kept of attendance, work achieved, and wage payments. Wages should be paid weekly or fortnightly if possible, to help staff with their cash needs; more frequent payment should be avoided, unless the situation is very unstable, because this incurs a great deal of administrative work.

Supervising construction teams
In a construction team the supervisor (foreman or team leader) has a very important role, which may include the following general areas of responsibility:

Hiring and firing: Although this can be open to abuse, if the supervisor is able to choose his or her team, they are likely to work well together, and the supervisor has a strong sanction if needed.

Daily administration: Checking attendance and preparing wage rolls, recording sickness and accidents, checking tools in and out of stores.

Staff supervision: Ensuring that the workers understand and can perform their tasks, that safety rules are followed, and that team problems are addressed; planning staff absences for collecting rations, where appropriate.

Technical supervision: Agreeing technical standards with senior technical staff and ensuring that those standards are met; ensuring that daily or weekly targets are met; reporting technical problems; giving technical guidance to workers, and on-the-job training if needed

Monitoring and reporting: Providing verbal or written records of progress for the programme monitoring system, to ensure that problems can be dealt with quickly and targets readjusted or resources increased as necessary.

A recommended number of workers per supervisor is 10–20. A site leader may, in turn, manage up to five supervisors.

5.2.5 Working with contractors

In some situations it may be appropriate to use contractors for tasks such as borehole drilling, latrine emptying, pipe laying, or latrine construction. In these cases a written and legally binding contract should be drawn up and signed by the programme manager and the contractor, which ensures that work is carried out to the correct standard, within budget and on time. There may be standard contract forms in the country of operation, or it may be necessary to design a contract, using a template to ensure that all necessary provisions are included.

5.2.6 Safety at work

Emergency settlements are often hazardous places to work, and many water-supply and sanitation activities involve an element of risk; for instance, erecting water tanks, spraying insecticides, or emptying latrines. Managers should ensure that staff, volunteers, and participants from the affected community are not put at undue risk because of their involvement on the project. They should provide protective clothing, supervise activities to reduce dangerous practice, provide first-aid kits, and ensure that field staff are trained in safe working practices, first aid, and procedures in case of accident. A common cause of injury is vehicle accidents; all necessary measures should be taken to avoid them, including enforcing the use of seatbelts.

Security may be an issue for staff working in the field, and water and sanitation plans should take this into account. For instance, where night-time curfews prevent the movement of staff, additional capacity for treating and storing water may need to be provided, in order to provide a day's supply during daylight hours. Every effort should be made to ensure that project activities do not put staff in danger, and that all staff are aware of security risks and procedures.

5.3 Administration

Most agencies have their own administrative procedures and systems that enable them to administer emergency programmes in field conditions, and these should be followed. The following points are intended as brief reminders of ways to help administrative and project systems to support each other.

5.3.1 Accounts and budget monitoring

Managers need up-to-date and reliable financial information to monitor spending to identify possible problems, check project progress against spending, anticipate possible shortfalls, and plan for budget revision if necessary. For this to be effective, accounts for spending in the field and for central spending need to be processed quickly and matched to give an overall picture of financial activity. The financial information needed may be quite detailed. For instance, it may be necessary to know how much is spent on several different activities in several different locations. In this case, receipts should be coded to identify the location and activity they relate to, and this code used throughout the accounting process. Field work in emergencies requires some cash to sort out small problems, such as buying a truck of sand or hiring casual labourers to unload a truck. A system of cash floats and accounting procedures is needed to speed up field operations and keep track of this spending. A stock-control system is another form of accounting.

5.3.2 Money (cash)

Cash is often a serious problem in emergency situations. Banking services may not be operating, and transferring large sums of cash for local spending presents serious problems of logistics and security. Field staff managing site work with large cash needs for wages or local purchases need to plan ahead and inform administrative staff well in advance of their cash needs. Wages administration can involve several staff involved in preparing and paying wages on site.

5.3.3 Personnel administration

Although a large number of staff at different levels may need to be hired rapidly to run an emergency programme, it is very important that records and administrative systems are set up to enable their payment, management, and welfare support to be administered efficiently. Standard systems can save time and help to avoid mistakes.

5.3.4 Co-ordinating administrative functions

It is most important to co-ordinate administrative functions, logistics, and project information to allow managers to keep track of what is happening and to keep spending and project activities under control. A great deal of money and goods can be lost if there are not reliable flows of information between the project, logistics, and administration, to avoid abuse and fraud, or simply to avoid overspending because of loss of control. Relief agencies can standardise and prepare in advance the paperwork needed to enable co-ordination between different administrative activities. Each transaction should be identified by date, activity, person responsible. and purchase order or order number, so that events can be retraced in case of problems.

Further reading

J. Davis and R. Lambert (1996) *Engineering in Emergencies: A practical guide for relief workers*, Chapter 5: 'Management', Chapter 6: 'Logistics', London: RedR/IT Publications

Part 3 | Technical Chapters

6 | Emergency settlements, site selection, and planning

6.1 Introduction

The number of people affected by disasters has multiplied several fold in recent years. It is estimated that in 1995 38 million people fled from conflicts, as refugees or internally displaced people, and more than 160 million people were affected by natural disasters. A large proportion of people affected by disasters spend at least part of the post-disaster period in temporary settlements, where living conditions and the constraints imposed by the location and nature of the settlement may have a huge impact on their well-being. There is a growing realisation of the problems caused by settling disaster-affected people in camps. Humanitarian agencies are beginning to consider a new approach to emergency settlements which takes a broad view of the needs of the disaster-affected community, while considering issues such as sustainability, environmental impact, social and economic impact, and security in the short and long terms. While UNHCR retains the mandate for site selection and site planning, humanitarian agencies responsible for sectoral activities must contribute to these processes, as issues critical to the success and effectiveness of temporary settlements are defined during this period.

The first section of the chapter looks at the processes and procedures of siting (section 6.2) and of establishing, extending, or upgrading (section 6.3) a temporary settlement. Most people affected by disasters, however, do not settle in sites which have been carefully selected and planned, but stay in unplanned or hastily chosen settlements. The final section in this chapter, section 6.4, therefore looks at the implications of settlement location and physical layout specific to water supply and sanitation.

6.2 Site selection

6.2.1 Introduction

There are three main options for humanitarian agencies to assist the settlement of disaster-affected populations: planned temporary settlements; supported self-settlement independent of planned settlements; and accommodation with host families or in rented accommodation. Care must be taken not to consider planned temporary settlements as the only or most appropriate response. It may be that the affected population would best be served by moving from one of these options to another, for example by stabilising people's health and re-grouping communities in a short-term planned settlement, before encouraging a move to supported, temporary self-settlement within a region.

It may be appropriate, necessary, and possible to settle the disaster-affected population on a site chosen for that purpose in a planned temporary settlement. The site may be a transit centre or camp, a semi-permanent camp, or an extension to an existing settlement or camp.

Site selection can be separated into the process that needs to be undertaken, detailed in the following section 6.2.2, and the procedure by which that process can be coordinated, detailed in section 6.2.3.

6.2.2 Site-selection process

The process is essentially in two stages:

- First, what type of settlement or settlements is required by the population, by the hosts, by the humanitarian agencies, and by security concerns?
- Second, what type of settlement or settlements is possible on the sites that are available, given physical constraints such as access, water supply, and topography?

Stage 1: the type of settlement required
There are a number of broad and interrelated considerations to take into account when selecting a site for settling an emergency-affected population. These considerations may be used to define what sort of settlement is desired or acceptable, how long it should be possible to remain in place, what sort of local impact it should have, etc. From this broad definition of a requirement, a set of more specific physical criteria can be used in the site-selection process to determine how the requirement can be met. Once site selection has taken place, the site planning of the settlement can take place (see section 6.3.1), on the basis of the requirements and physical limitations defined.

The broad considerations described below can be used to inform the site-selection requirement by quantifying the importance of each in relation to the other, through appropriate assessments (see section 6.2.3), to define a set of requirements.

Security: Security for the affected community, the local community, and for project staff is influenced by settlement location in relation to the presence of local communities, borders, or fighting forces. The size and layout of a settlement may have an influence on violence within the affected community. People from within the emergency settlement may pose a threat to others outside it, and vice versa.

Sustainability: Many disasters produce long-term settlements of displaced people, though there may be a reluctance to recognise this on the part of everyone concerned, for many reasons. A long-term view is needed to ensure that people affected by the disaster can live healthy and dignified lives over a long period, without creating undue problems for local people. Planning for sustainability requires consideration of other issues such as security, protection, access, environmental concerns, the local context, attitudes of the host authority and donors, and the nature of the displaced population.

Social cohesion: This can be influenced by the location, size, and layout of the emergency settlement. Large, isolated, and dense settlements without a clear spatial definition of local areas may create tensions and disorientation and make community rebuilding more difficult.

Relationship with local communities: The degree to which settlements are integrated with or separated from local communities influences social relations, local markets for labour and goods, political developments, security, and sustainability. It is important to be aware of the relative numbers of directly affected people and the host communities, and their relative assets.

Example: an affected rural community from the Great Lakes region of central Africa moves into a neighbouring country, which has a high population density. The local population is generally sympathetic to the affected population, but there are few blood ties, and the situation is very politicised. Small vacated sites exist in the country of asylum, once used for previous displaced populations. Ideally, the form of temporary settlement for a rural population might be low-density and dispersed, to support maximum self-sufficiency. Security concerns, however, mean that the first priority is to site the settlement away from the border and to ensure protection. Assessments of both the local and refugee communities suggest that it is possible to have limited contact between the communities, so the recommended requirement is for a series of small relatively dense camps, away from the border, possibly on the old sites. The next stage is to assess the old sites to determine whether they are suitable.

Stage 2: the type of settlement possible
The second and final stage of the site-selection process is to test the requirements for the temporary settlement against physical considerations for each potential site.

Water: Water must be made available in suitable quantities and of suitable quality throughout the year. Extraction must not adversely affect the environment or local populace.

Space: Sufficient land area must be available for the desired population density. Topography must allow for habitation, yet also surface-water drainage. The soil type must be suited to habitation and, where required, should support appropriate forms of agriculture or livestock.

Environment: A sufficient and sustainable supply of timber for fuel and construction is required for the affected population, or mitigating programmes will be needed. Other environmental considerations include climate, the pollution of ground-water, and the presence of endemic vectors.

Example: sufficient old sites with suitable resources are found, although there will not be sufficient timber for fuel or construction in the area, and improvements to water supply are needed. A regional fuel-wood programme can be put in place, shelter systems can be assembled from materials purchased regionally, and the improvements to the water supply will offer benefits to the local population. Unused land that can be reclaimed for agriculture is identified near the sites. Additional influxes are seen as likely, and refugees residing with host families are concerned that they will not be able to remain for much longer, so another site is identified nearer the border for a transit and reception centre. When this proposal is presented to refugees, they complain that the old sites have associations with oppressive policies. Discussions with UNHCR and the local government produce the assurances that the refugees were looking for. The planning of the sites is begun.

6.2.3 Site-selection procedure

Site selection in practice is a difficult process, requiring a number of immediate and long-term considerations to be weighed up, in a situation of great uncertainty, with conflicting priorities to be taken into account. Decisions taken about site location during the early days of an emergency situation have long-term implications, and there may be tremendous pressure to take decisions rapidly. Assessments of the populations and sites involved are therefore essential and should be undertaken to the limit of the time and resources available. It is helpful for the decision-making process to use a systematic approach when comparing possible options. There are bound to be various, potentially conflicting sectoral priorities involved, and so a joint decision-making process should be used, which allows all the significant issues to be considered in an open way. The approach described below attempts to clarify issues and priorities at the start of the process and then to follow an objective system to arrive at a quantified comparison of sites according to those issues and priorities already agreed.

1. Agree issues to be addressed in Stage 1 of the site-selection process, such as security, possible duration, dependency/self-sufficiency, programme costs, integration with/segregation from local host population, urgency of decision, likely future population movements, political and security issues, and social, legal, and cultural issues. In other words, agree on the priorities concerning the settlement or the affected community to produce a requirement for the settlement.

2. Agree a list of criteria in Stage 2 of the site-selection process which will have an impact on these issues, such as topography and location, soil type, water sources, land area available, access, vegetation, fuel-wood, environmental impact of settlement and service delivery, and environmental health hazards.

3. Prioritise criteria according to their relevance to the key issues to be addressed (point 1), and agree a method of weighting which reflects these priorities.

4. Determine the site and population characteristics through site visits and assessments. These assessments should include the following:

   - *Disaster-affected community profile:* Identify social and ethnic make-up, gender and age distributions, traditional and current livelihoods, health status and disease risks, political and conflict-related issues.
   - *Local population profile:* Describe a similar profile of the local population. In addition a basic local and regional economic profile should be used, to identify sources of materials, areas of potential conflict of interest between disaster-affected community and local people, existing development initiatives, and local services.
   - *Environmental and resource survey:* Assess the long-term availability and management of local natural resources, such as water, fuel, and construction timber, and livestock fodder. Try to predict the potential impacts of the disaster-affected population on the environment, such as soil erosion from deforestation, and the creation of areas of standing water. Assess the immediate and long-term environmental health risks due to local prevalence of disease and the presence of disease vectors and their breeding sites.

5. Rank the sites. Once the criteria and weightings have been agreed and the assessments carried out, the sites can be compared. Some criteria may be so critical to the outcomes required (point 1) that they effectively rule out that site. For instance, a site prone to severe seasonal flooding would simply not meet the requirements for duration if it is anticipated or desired that the site will be in place for more than a few weeks. On the other hand, short-term security considerations may over-ride the issue of flooding.

6.2.4 Responsibilities of water-supply and sanitation staff

Staff responsible for water supply and sanitation should be involved in the site-selection process at certain of these selection stages, as follows:

Listing and weighting key criteria: Ensure that topography, soil type, water sources, space available, access, vegetation, environmental impact, and environmental health hazards are given sufficient weighting. The technical challenges and cost implications of providing water, sanitation, and shelter on unsuitable sites are often not appreciated by people without specialist knowledge in these areas.

Determining site characteristics: Water and sanitation specialists should be involved in the assessment process, to ensure that the characteristics of the site relating to these activities are properly understood and an appropriate score given to each of the criteria which are relevant. The assessment questions listed in Chapter 1 can be used as a means of checking that all the main points relevant to water supply and sanitation are addressed in the assessment of the site.

Ranking the sites and choice of site: In practice, this is usually a process of negotiation, readjustment of criteria, and last-minute lobbying or pressure from various sources. Water-supply and sanitation specialists should ensure that criteria which effectively rule out certain sites are applied and not ignored, and that objective assessments and analyses are not discounted for reasons which are broadly political and not made explicit at the beginning of the process. The implications of the choice should still be made very clear, and efforts made to ensure that the decision-making process is as transparent as possible and that responsibility for unsuitable site selection is identified.

6.2.5 Decision-making

In many cases the site-selection process happens at a time when the affected population is already settled on a temporary site, and the costs of moving to a better site have to taken into account. The costs of moving people and programmes are often overstated in relation to the long-term benefits. There is often a tendency for agencies which have invested in the original site to give a high weighting to the costs of closing down their existing facilities and starting again on new sites. The psycho-social problems for the affected people who have begun to settle should not be ignored. This should be counterbalanced by giving a realistic weighting to the advantages of moving. The longer the decision is left, the greater are the costs of moving, and the less likely it is that the site will be changed. There is sometimes a very short period of days or weeks during which it is possible to make a decision before unsuitable sites become semi-permanent, with long-term consequences for the welfare of the affected population, local people, the local environment, and programme costs.

Decisions on site selection often tend to be made by a small group of technicians, managers, administrators, and politicians, with very little consultation with the affected community. This may be partly because the decision is politically sensitive and has to be taken rapidly. But given that site selection has such a major impact on the health and welfare of the affected community, a more consultative process should be sought.

6.3 Physical planning of emergency settlements

Where new sites are selected, or existing sites extended or reorganised, water-supply and sanitation staff should be involved in the physical planning process to ensure that the settlement created is a healthy environment in which to live and carry out essential activities effectively. The Sphere Guidelines (see 'Further reading' at the end of this chapter) attach indicators to standards which quantify some of the points below.

6.3.1 Site-planning process

Attention should be given to the following points in particular. These apply whether a new site or an extension to an existing site is being laid out, or an existing site is being improved by rearranging living and service areas, and providing more space by moving some dwellings to a new site or to the periphery.

Water supply

- The population settled on the site should be no more than can be supplied by the water available.
- Shelters and latrines should be located so as to avoid contaminating water sources.
- Space should be available for water points in areas which allow drainage of waste water and where contamination is not a significant risk.
- Space should be available for water storage/treatment facilities and pipe routes.
- It should be possible to supply water to all areas of the site cost-effectively and without serious technical complications.

Excreta disposal

- Land for toilets should be available sufficiently close to shelters. The size and location of latrine blocks should be determined by the culture of the affected population, which will determine the way in which latrines are used and the best way in which maintenance can be agreed. Enough land should be available to allow latrines to be sited at least 6 metres from shelters and sufficiently far from water points to avoid contamination.
- On sites with varied soil type and topography, there must be suitable land distributed throughout the site for latrines.

- Land should be available for excreta-disposal measures such as latrines and off-site disposal (which reduces the risk of contaminating the environment surrounding the site).
- Access to latrines and septic tanks for emptying must be possible.

Solid-waste management

- Key waste-producing points such as markets, abattoirs, and health facilities should be located so as to facilitate refuse management and reduce the risk of contaminating the site.
- Suitable space should be available on or off the site for final disposal of solid waste. It should be located to avoid causing a nuisance or health hazard to the affected community or local people.
- Access to solid-waste collection points should be possible, using the appropriate means (wheelbarrow, handcart, animal cart, or truck).

Burial grounds

- Allow space for up to three graves per 1,000 people per month, outside residential areas of the settlement, downstream and at least 50m from ground-water sources.
- Check preferences for the location of burial grounds with the affected community.

Vector control

- Living areas should be located as far as necessary from permanent or seasonal vector-breeding sites to reduce people's exposure to an acceptable level.
- Sufficient living space should be allowed to keep vector-borne disease related to overcrowding to an acceptable level.

Drainage

- Living areas and service areas and structures should be located so as to reduce the risk of their flooding and so as to facilitate disposal of any run-off and waste water they may produce.
- Settled areas of the site should be located on land which meets minimum standards concerning slope, vegetation cover, etc.

Hygiene promotion

- The layout of the site and the number of people settled on the site should enable social cohesion and reduce forces producing conflict within the community and between the affected community and local people.
- The layout of the camp should allow social and administrative structures to have a spatial expression, to facilitate contacts with the affected population.
- The layout of the settlement should be such that hygiene-related problems are kept to a minimum.

6.4 Settlement location and physical layout: implications for water supply and sanitation

The most important feature of any emergency settlement is the disaster-affected community itself. (See Chapter 1 for a discussion of disaster-affected communities.) The most important physical characteristics of emergency settlements are their location, population size, layout, and population density. Location determines many factors: physical factors, such as access to water, environmental health risks, climate, soil type, and topography; and also non-physical factors, such as security, self-sufficiency, and contact with local communities. In un-planned camps, population density is largely a product of population size and physical layout of the settlement. In planned camps, population density and the dispersal of populations into a number of camps can be used to optimise the physical and non-physical factors of location mentioned above. The major implications of all these factors for water supply and sanitation are summarised in Table 6.1.

Table 6.1 Major implications of settlement location, population size, and physical layout for water supply and sanitation

	Feature of settlement		
Sector	Location	Population size and culture	Layout and population density
Water supply	Quantity of water available	Quantity of water needed	Possible pipe routes
	Distance to water sources	Scale of response required	Space for water points and drainage
	Quality of water available and need for treatment	Large populations are more dependent on central systems	Number and distribution of taps
	Possible sources of contamination	Cultural aspects of the distribution of water for washing, laundry, and anal cleansing all have impacts on the planning of the camp	Provision for livestock or agriculture
	Access for local people to the water supply		Back-up capacity in distribution systems
	Effects on local water supplies		
	Variety of sources and therefore security		
	Seasonal hazards such as flooding		

Table 6.1 Major implications of settlement location, population size, and physical layout for water supply and sanitation (continued)

	Feature of settlement		
Sector	**Location**	**Population size and culture**	**Layout and population density**
Excreta disposal	Soil type Climate Water-table depth Slope Availability of local materials Possible contamination of water supplies Impact on local environment Seasonal hazards such as flooding	Impact on local environment Supplies of local materials Possible pollution by off-site excreta disposal Latrine-block sizes determined by maintenance options, influenced by culture and density	Space available for on-site disposal systems Zones for locating toilets or defecation areas Access for latrine emptying if needed Access to latrines, especially by women and at night Access to the bush for defecation
Solid-waste management	Type and quantity of resources brought into the settlement, and type and quantity of waste produced Soil type for possible on-site burial Location of off-site discharge Environmental impact	Amount of refuse to be disposed of Number of waste-collection points Likely need for a centralised collection system Size of markets, health centres, and other sources of solid waste	Location and number of waste-collection points Space available for on-site disposal Access for solid-waste collection Effect of smoke from burning refuse Siting cemeteries
Vector control	Prevalent vectors and vector-borne diseases Breeding sites already present Environmental impact of vector-control programme	Number of people exposed to an outbreak of vector-borne disease Level of support available for vector-control programme	Proximity of vector-breeding sites to certain areas of the settlement Density and movements of vectors Breeding sites within the settlement Movement of vectors between settlements

Table 6.1 Major implications of settlement location, population size, and physical layout for water supply and sanitation (continued)

	Feature of settlement		
Sector	Location	Population size and culture	Layout and population density
Drainage	Soil type, vegetation cover, rainfall, slope, flooding	Number of shelters and volume of water to be drained from site	Drainage courses, roads, and open spaces Location of water points and other sources of waste water
Hygiene promotion	Hygiene problems to be addressed Security	Social structures (already in place or developing) Social cohesion and conflict	Hygiene problems to be addressed

Further reading

M. B. Anderson (1994) *People-oriented Planning at Work: Using PoP to Improve UNHCR Programming*, Geneva: UNHCR

A. Chalinder (1998) *Temporary Human Settlement Planning for Displaced Populations in Emergencies*, RRN Good Practice Review 6, London: ODI

J. Davis and R. Lambert, (1995) *Engineering in Emergencies: A practical guide for relief workers*, Chapter 17, London: RedR/IT Publications

UNHCR (1982, revision currently awaiting publication) *Handbook for Emergencies*, Geneva: UNHCR

7 | Hygiene promotion

7.1 Introduction

7.1.1 Hygiene and health

A number of studies have suggested that the impact of hygiene practices on water-related and sanitation-related disease can be as great as that of improvements in water supply and sanitation. Hygiene behaviour is a critical influence on the transmission of disease at various stages. A primary barrier is safe defecation, to prevent faecal pathogens entering the human environment. A secondary barrier is hand-washing, to ensure that faecal contamination on hands is not transmitted via food or water. Each of a thousand daily actions taken by ordinary people may encourage or discourage the transmission of disease. This is particularly important in emergency situations where disease risks are acute due to overcrowding, poor water and sanitation, exposure to new pathogens, low resistance to disease, and disturbance of familiar and safe habits.

7.1.2 Influencing hygiene practice

Influencing hygiene practice is widely considered to be an essential element of an effective water-supply and sanitation response to emergencies. However, it is difficult to measure the impact of such programmes in emergency situations, and the evidence of their success in emergencies is limited. Nevertheless, it is possible to assess, plan, and implement effective hygiene-promotion activities in emergency situations, as long as this is done with clear objectives that are focused on a very small number of important practices that can be rapidly influenced. The purpose of this chapter is to encourage a planned approach to encouraging improved hygiene practice, together with improvements in water supplies and sanitation. Methods used for identifying hygiene risks and influencing behaviour are drawn from a wide range of disciplines, and the essential qualities of hygiene-promotion workers are their ability to communicate and to take a broad approach to tackling hygiene problems.

Most of the material for this chapter was taken from Oxfam's internal Guidelines for Hygiene Promotion in Emergencies, written by Suzanne Ferron, and large parts of that manual are reproduced or adapted here.

7.1.3 Definition of hygiene promotion in emergencies

Hygiene promotion may be defined as follows.

- It is the planned and systematic attempt to enable people to take action to prevent illness related to water and sanitation, and to maximise the benefits of improved water and sanitation facilities.
- It combines 'insider' knowledge (what beneficiaries know, do, and want) with 'outsider' knowledge (such as the causes of diarrhoeal diseases, communications and learning strategies, and evaluations of previous water and sanitation projects).
- It includes the provision of information and learning opportunities regarding aspects of personal and environmental hygiene, including water provision, excreta disposal, drainage, solid-waste disposal, and vector control (more commonly known as Hygiene Education).
- It makes better hygiene possible in an emergency by providing essential items that may be in short supply, such as storage containers for water and food, soap, and sanitary protection.
- It provides the crucial link between people in the community and the technical interventions.
- It enables the community to participate in planning and implementing programmes, and informs the community of agencies' plans and activities.

Hygiene promotion has a narrower focus than health promotion, but both aim to promote positive health and to enable people to take action to prevent illness.

7.1.4 Focus of hygiene promotion in emergencies

Hygiene promotion may be used to help disaster-affected people to avoid and limit the extraordinary hygiene risks created by the disaster situation (overcrowding, poor sanitation etc.); and to understand and use new facilities (public toilets, chlorinated water, etc.) In addition, community mobilisation to encourage participation in water-supply and sanitation projects is commonly included in hygiene-promotion activities.

The objectives of hygiene-promotion activities should be considered carefully, in order to avoid distorting key messages, confusing people, or sending messages to the wrong people. The understanding gained through assessing hygiene risks should be used to plan and prioritise material assistance, so that information flows usefully between the agency and the people concerned.

High-risk hygiene practices

Commonly the two most important aspects of hygiene practice are safe disposal of faeces, and washing hands with soap (or some alternative) after contact with faeces (defecation or handling children's stools). These are likely to be the two most important practices for hygiene-promotion programmes to target. In most emergency situations, other practices such as covering food or burying refuse are likely to be of secondary importance. However, it may be that some types of behaviour are easier to address than others. For example, in a situation where people affected by a disaster have never used toilets before and there is a high level of faecal contamination in the environment, it may be more effective to ensure that people are supplied with suitable containers for drinking water, soap for washing hands, and fuel for thorough heating of food than to expect people to adapt rapidly to using latrines. An assessment is needed to determine which key practices to address and the likely prospects of influencing them. This assessment should look at resources available to the beneficiaries as well as their hygiene practices, so that messages do not promote unrealistic change.

Promoting use of facilities

Where people suddenly have to use facilities they are not familiar with, such as defecation fields, they need clear information and encouragement to use them correctly. Communication is a two-way process, and users should have the opportunity to feed their opinions back into the programme.

Promoting participation in programmes

Promotional activities may also be needed in support of programmes such as constructing family latrines or managing refuse. Without the understanding and participation of the people concerned, these programmes are unlikely to succeed. 'Participation' has several meanings here, including participation in decision-making and programme design, accepting and supporting the programme, and contributing time, labour, money, or materials to a programme. Participation should be encouraged for the purpose of sharing responsibility and ownership, rather than saving money, and should be sensitive to gender issues and other social considerations. Participation that creates additional burdens for women and does not include them in decision making is quite contrary to the meaning of the word as it is used here.

7.2 Assessment

7.2.1 Initial assessment

Briefly assess key hygiene practices relating to disease risk. In a concentrated settlement, this should take no more than two or three days. Use rapid assessment methods initially: exploratory walks; focus groups (men, women, and children);

discussions with key informants and opinion leaders (such as secular and religious leaders, elders, teachers, and traditional birth attendants). See Chapter 2 for notes on these techniques.

In the initial assessment period, try to identify community structures and leaders. Social structures may have become severely disrupted during an emergency and may now be non-existent. If the community is able to regroup and elect or nominate new leaders, this will facilitate any future work with them. If water supplies and sanitation facilities are to be installed or rehabilitated, try to assess existing or possible mechanisms for future maintenance, such as water committees or user groups. Outreach workers may already exist, and their initial training may simply need to be supplemented: try to identify them. It is also useful to try to find out what media of communication are most common in the community, and whether there are existing tools and visual aids that might be used by the outreach workers. People with expertise in public health or community development may be available in the community; try to identify them. During the initial assessment, try to identify other potential people to work with who might be involved in a campaign or who could be attendants at water points or latrines. Find out what previous hygiene-promotion initiatives people have been exposed to, as this may influence the emergency programme activities.

7.2.2 Longer-term assessment

Continue with a more detailed assessment as you design and implement your campaign or the first phase of your project. Other participatory methods of assessment, such as pocket charts and mapping, may be used, once the facilitators have received appropriate follow-up training in how to use these techniques. A structured observation exercise may be useful in order to provide some quantitative data for monitoring and evaluation purposes. Aim to have completed this within three months. Always make sure that feedback is provided to the community.

Large questionnaire surveys are time-consuming and expensive; they require specialised knowledge of survey design to provide valid information. When discussing hygiene, people may give the answers they think you want to hear, thus making the results unreliable. Only use a survey if you are confident of your design and sampling methods and the relevance and validity of the data you hope to obtain.

7.3 Setting objectives and choosing indicators

The assessment process should identify the major hygiene problems to be addressed. Some of these problems should be solved by the improvement of water supplies and sanitation. Others may need hygiene-education work to enable safer hygiene practice.

Objectives for hygiene promotion should be set in the same way as for other water-supply and sanitation activities, and they should include indicators for monitoring progress. Objectives should be SMART (see section 3.1), and the indicators, derived from assessment information, should be monitored as a part of normal project implementation, as far as possible. See section 4.1.

Hygiene-promotion needs are likely to change frequently during the project period, as hygiene practices change, and access to water supplies and sanitation evolves. Objectives and indicators should be revised periodically on the basis of monitoring information, or as a response to new developments.

7.4 Implementation

7.4.1 Hygiene education

Target all sections of the population where appropriate: men, women, and children. It may be useful to recruit people who have a specific responsibility to work with children. Where schools are functioning or there are opportunities for non-formal education, it may be possible to support or introduce a hygiene-promotion component into the syllabus.

If a campaign approach is chosen, it should focus on a few key messages and should achieve its objectives within about two weeks. There may be a need for further campaigns if there is a sudden deterioration in the situation and/or an outbreak of disease. However, campaigns that persist indicate that it is not possible to achieve the desired changes fast enough to have an impact on the emergency situation, or that the methods used are ineffective. In these cases a more participatory approach would be better. Consider providing information at registration areas, distribution points, water sources, market places, and any other public areas. Consider using a loudspeaker system, radio if available, short dramas, songs and/or puppet shows. Where possible, always give the public the opportunity to ask questions.

We know from development programmes that message-based hygiene education has only a limited ability to change behaviour. It is a common fallacy that people are empty vessels into which knowledge, leading to behavioural change, can be poured. The dissemination of messages, especially if repeated frequently, however, can help to raise awareness about a particular issue or may simply provide information.

7.4.2 Staff

Outreach workers of some form will be required to work with community members. These workers may be identified by the project or by the community, taking into account the following criteria: literacy and numeracy, gender, ethnicity, age, and, most importantly, attitude towards other people. Discussions with community members may help you to decide some of these issues; but where time is limited, rapid identification will be necessary.

Outreach workers may already be available and should be identified in your initial assessment. If you decide that a campaign is necessary, you will need to provide a short two-day training course for the campaign workers and ensure that their activities are supervised closely. It will be of benefit if short meetings are organised in the course of the campaign to assess any major problems. The numbers of workers will depend on the area to be covered and its accessibility.

Recruit additional workers as soon as possible, and plan or adapt training courses. One worker is recommended per thousand people, but it may be necessary to review this number, depending on workload, population density, and accessibility. You may also want to recruit workers to collect data from structured observations.

Initially, workers should concentrate on a few key issues, such as excreta disposal and hand-washing practices. Then, once the excreta-disposal programme is under way, begin to look in more detail at methods of collecting and storing water, vector control, disposal of solid waste, and drainage.

7.4.3 Co-ordination

Some projects may focus on short-term improvement of water supplies. If this is the case, try to align implementation with the technical intervention. Identifying water sources and prioritising those to be protected or rehabilitated should be undertaken jointly by technical and hygiene-promotion staff.

Defecation fields or public latrines are often the most appropriate option in the absence of any sanitation system, but together with the sanitation engineer you will need to design a longer-term system. This should take account of what the community feels is appropriate, and cater to the needs of adults and children and those with special requirements, such as the sick or disabled.

Liaison with other medical agencies is important, to ensure an overview of the health situation and to obtain data from any epidemiological surveillance that may be in operation. Information gained from discussion groups with community members should also be shared with their permission with other agencies.

Programmes or interventions run by other agencies or by the host government will often contain some component of hygiene promotion, whether this involves plans to distribute soap or to develop a cholera-preparedness strategy, so liaison with them is vital.

Health agencies may want to set up a system of outreach workers who will be involved in case-finding and basic health education. However, there is a tendency for hygiene and health education to become marginalised when outreach staff are also engaged in case-finding or basic treatment, and it is preferable for the hygiene promoters to devote their time to water and sanitation issues. Close liaison with other agencies is necessary, to discuss these issues and to ensure that activities are co-ordinated and that consistent messages are given.

Table 7.1 Sample project plan

Activity	Week numbers											
	1	2	3	4	5	6	7	8	9	10	11	12
1 Initial assessment	■											
2 Construct trench latrines		■	■									
3 Recruit and train latrine and water-point attendants: 2 per installation	■											
4 Provide hand-washing facilities: 2 per installation	■	■										
5 Recruit and train 20 campaign workers		■										
Campaign												
6 Distribute hygiene kits		■	■									
7 Recruit and train 10 children's hygiene-promotion workers			■	■								
8 Recruit and train 30 more hygiene-promotion workers				■	■	■						
Participatory hygiene promotion												
9 Provide 7–20 litres of water per day	■	■	■	■	■	■	■	■	■	■	■	■
10 Ensure adequate shower and laundry facilities					■	■	■	■	■	■	■	■
11 Liaise with other agencies in the camp	■	■	■	■	■	■	■	■	■	■	■	■
12 On-going assessment, planning and monitoring	■	■	■	■	■	■	■	■	■	■	■	■
13 Identify and train workers to carry out structured observation					■	■						

The incidence of diarrhoea will depend on many factors which may not be under your direct control. The availability and quality of food, shelter, and medical care will all affect morbidity and mortality rates and advocacy. Inter-agency liaison regarding these may also be a part of hygiene promotion.

7.4.4 Communication methods

Discussion groups, puppet shows, plays, and songs, followed by questions and discussion, are probably more cost-effective than visits to individual homes or shelters; but people may not always want to join in with group discussions, or they may be available only at certain times. Women especially may be too busy to attend discussion groups. A combination of approaches is probably best.

Table 7.1 on page 105 shows how hygiene promotion activities may be planned and implemented as part of a water-supply and sanitation programme.

Box 7.1 Hygiene-promotion actions that could be taken in an acute emergency

- Recruit and train public-latrine attendants to ensure cleaning and maintenance of public latrines and to encourage hand-washing following use of latrines. (People won't use dirty, smelly latrines.)
- Train water-source attendants to encourage people not to defecate near to water sources.
- Recruit and train facilitators/outreach workers to mobilise the community to dig family latrines.
- Organise the distribution of hygiene kits (including soap, water containers, food storage containers, and cloths).
- Cordon off water sources that are suspected of being contaminated with cholera. Train watchmen to do this and to explain to people why it is necessary.
- Recruit and train campaign workers to provide key information to people over a period of one to two weeks.
- Train support workers to chlorinate all wells and to test for residual chlorine levels.
- Identify appropriate siting of tap-stands through discussions with engineers and community members.
- Enlist the support of community leaders through discussions with them about the project.
- Liaise with other agencies to determine possible collaboration on hygiene promotion.
- Attend co-ordination meetings with other agencies and provide feedback on refugees' expressed concerns.
- Discuss with community members the issue of corralling animals and how this might be facilitated.
- During an outbreak of diarrhoeal disease (including cholera), keep the community informed of the extent and severity of the outbreak and the benefits of reporting cases promptly.

7.5 Programme monitoring

A common weakness of emergency hygiene-promotion programmes is that activities are planned and then implemented without a clear indication that they have any impact on behaviour or health. It is most important that each element in an emergency water-supply and sanitation programme can be demonstrated to be effective, when scarce resources have to be shared among various programme areas. Hygiene-promotion activities which do not address real problems, or which misinform or confuse the affected population, may do more harm than good. Monitoring is therefore an essential part of a hygiene-promotion project. It should be done, as far as possible, by means of normal programme activities for data collection; but it may be necessary to carry out a survey to gather information on a specific aspect of hygiene, such as the way water is used in the household, and this may be done with the same techniques used for assessment (see section 2.2).

7.6 Training

Training activities and methodologies should be planned to meet project objectives. Training sessions will need to take account of how many people are to be trained, the length of the training, who will do it, where it will be held, what methods will be used, how it will be evaluated, and the arrangements for follow up training and support.

The number of people to be trained will depend on the methodologies used. Training sessions that rely on the active participation of trainees become difficult if the group size exceeds 20–25 people; they generally work best with 8–10 people. When working with larger groups, ensure that there is ample opportunity for small-group work.

If you are expecting people to attend promptly for the whole course, then you will probably need to pay them for their attendance. Both men and women may incur costs if they have to attend training at the expense of their other responsibilities. Training should be timed to fit in with domestic and other activities.

Ideally training should be conducted in the participants' mother tongue. It may be useful to arrange a short training for trainers to focus on how people learn best, and the use of participatory teaching methods.

Ensure that a meeting is arranged following the first day of the campaign, to allow facilitators to voice any concern or problems they encountered. Further follow-up meetings should be arranged on a regular basis with all facilitators.

Supervisory visits to field workers should also be scheduled, and extra supervisors may be needed, either as separate appointments or chosen or elected from the existing facilitators.

Those involved in collecting structured observations will require careful supervision and follow up, to ensure that forms are filled out accurately to avoid observer bias and inconsistency.

7.7 Community management

Experience has shown that the long-term maintenance of water and sanitation installations should always be taken into account, even in emergency situations. This is especially important where permanent water supplies are being constructed or renovated. People will not automatically assume the responsibility for keeping the system functional in the longer term; they may think that this will be taken care of by the agency concerned. The community may well have 'participated' in construction work, but this does not automatically mean that they feel a sense of ownership of the completed project. It is important to consider the following points:

- Do people in the community consider that the project responds to their own priority needs?
- Have women been involved as far as possible in the initial discussions on the proposed project?
- Are men and women in a position to devote time and effort to maintaining facilities? How can the burden be shared?
- Does the project have the support of local government and community leaders? If respected community leaders are available, they (rather than the agency) should lead the discussions.
- Ensure that the issue of long-term maintenance is raised as soon as possible with community groups. Ask them how they intend to repair the system if it breaks down, or what provision they have made for this in the past. Ensure that issues of financial accountability are also discussed. The availability of spare parts for pumps or other systems will also need to be investigated and viable systems identified.
- If people do not attend meetings, try to find out why, and whether alternative arrangements can be made.
- Try to ensure open and on-going dialogue about the project. It is important to remain flexible and to encourage suggestions from community members on how the project should proceed.
- Formal agreements and contracts should be drafted when discussions have been finalised.

Further reading

A. Almedom, U. Blumenthal, and L. Manderson (1997) *Hygiene Evaluation Procedures: Approaches and methods for assessing water and sanitation related practices,* Boston: International Nutrition Foundation for Developing Countries (INFCD)

M. Boot (1991) *Just Stir Gently: The way to mix hygiene education with water supply and sanitation,* The Hague: IRC

CARE Hygiene Promotion Manual for the Great Lakes, unpublished

S. Ferron (1998) Oxfam Guidelines for Hygiene Promotion in Emergencies, Oxford: Oxfam (unpublished, not for general circulation)

J. Hubley (1993) *Communicating Health: an action guide to health education and health promotion*, Basingstoke: Macmillan

Sphere Project (1999, forthcoming) *Humanitarian Charter and Minimum Standards in Disaster Response*, Chapter 2, section 7, 'Hygiene Promotion', published in Geneva by the Steering Committee for Humanitarian Response (SCHR) and Interaction; e-mail: sphere@ifrc.org; internet: *www.sphereproject.org*

8 | Water supply

8.1 Introduction

8.1.1 Water quantity and access

The amount of water that people need for a healthy life varies greatly between different peoples, between times of the year, days of the week, and particular circumstances. Nomadic people displaced in Somaliland in 1992 had long-standing water-use habits based on just 2 to 3 litres per person per day (lcd). Kurdish refugees from cities in Northern Iraq had been used to at least 100 litres per person per day. During the days before they left the camps in eastern Turkey to return home, water consumption rose dramatically, as people washed bedding and clothes in preparation for the return. In the camps of Rwandan refugees in Eastern Zaire, water consumption increased on Saturdays as clothes were washed and chores done before resting on Sundays. Providing water for animals may also be essential for health. If it is not provided, people will consume less themselves, or their animals will not thrive and their livelihoods will suffer. If there is inadequate provision for animals, there may be conflict over the use of water sources. Table 8.1 gives suggested planning figures for meeting water needs in addition to the minimum required for drinking, cooking, and domestic and personal hygiene.

Water should be available sufficiently close to where people are living for them to be able to collect it easily, and sufficient water points are needed to allow access for all. See Chapter 2 of the *Humanitarian Charter and Minimum Standards in Disaster Relief*, produced by the Sphere Project, for guidance on minimum water quantity and access. Details are given in 'Further reading' at the end of this chapter.

Table 8.1 Water quantities in addition to the minimum required for drinking, cooking and personal hygiene

Public toilets	1–2 litres/user/day for hand-washing
	2–8 litres/user/day for cleaning toilet
All flushing toilets	20–40 litres/user/day for conventional flushing toilets
	3–5 litres/user/day for pour-flush toilets
Anal washing	1–2 litres/person/day
Health centres and hospitals	5 litres/outpatient
	40–60 litres/in-patient/day
	Additional quantities may be needed for some laundry equipment, flushing toilets, etc.
Cholera centres	60 litres/patient/day
	15 litres/carer/day if appropriate
Therapeutic feeding centres	15–30 litres/patient/day
	15 litres/carer/day if appropriate
Livestock	20–30 litres/large or medium animal/day
	5 litres/small animal/day

8.1.2 Water quality

The World Health Organisation (WHO) guidelines on drinking-water quality recommend that water for human consumption should be absolutely free of faecal contamination and should conform to limits on chemical contaminants. In most emergency situations the greatest short-term risk to public health is posed by faecal contamination rather than by chemical contamination. Water quality becomes more important where the population figures and/or population densities are high, and where there is a risk of water-related and excreta-related epidemic disease.

In cases such as disasters following industrial accidents, the chemical water quality may be of prime concern. In the long term, the chemical composition of water may have significant effects on health, and this should be considered. See Chapter 2 of the Sphere Project *Minimum Standards* for water-quality indicators in emergencies. These refer to short-term supplies. WHO guidelines must be used for choosing and managing long-term supplies.

8.1.3 Decisions about quantity and quality

If there are choices to be made about increasing water quantity or improving water quality when time and resources are scarce, priority should always be given to increasing the *quantity* of water available, even if the water provided is contaminated. Water with up to 100 faecal coliforms per 100 ml (see section 8.10.3) may be provided for a very short period in an emergency, until treatment systems are in place. In many emergencies, the most important routes for the transmission of water- and excreta-related disease are linked to hygiene problems caused by insufficient quantity of water, rather than by contaminated water supplies. It should be stressed, however, that every effort should be made at this stage to protect water supplies from contamination and to provide facilities for safe defecation, particularly at times of water-related and excreta-related epidemics, to reduce the risk of water-borne disease transmission.

8.2 Planning and implementation

8.2.1 Introduction

Although many emergency water-supply interventions develop into construction projects, they may start with improvised systems, or simply workers posted at river banks adding chlorine to buckets as the water is collected. Initial arrangements are usually replaced later on if the population is settled for some months, and more permanent systems can be constructed. The most appropriate source of water for large populations is usually a surface source, such as a river or lake, because, although this will need treating, it is available in sufficient quantity straight away. Water from springs and existing wells may not be sufficient, and new wells may take weeks or even months to dig or drill. Surface water is treated and distributed via pipes and taps. Ground water is also often treated with chlorine, to ensure that it remains safe to drink after collection. The quality of the system installed depends on the likely life-span of the settlement and the willingness of authorities or agencies to invest resources in more permanent systems. The design and construction of water systems may demand specialist skills and equipment, such as drilling rigs, but most work is possible with basic equipment and technical skills. Regular maintenance is needed to keep systems running satisfactorily, particularly those involving pumps and other mechanical equipment, and this becomes an increasingly important activity as time goes on. Monitoring of water quality may be necessary, as well as monitoring water consumption, to ensure that the system continues to provide what it was designed to provide.

Labourers and technicians from the disaster-affected community usually do most of the construction work and subsequent maintenance of the systems. Externally recruited engineers and, occasionally, specialists such as hydro-geologists or pollution experts may be needed at some stages of the programme. Where urban water-supply systems need repairs and/or rehabilitation, specialist engineers will also be needed. In many situations, though, much of the work can be done with local skills: most emergency work using simple lightweight equipment does not need formal training in engineering. In many situations, experienced engineers and technicians are present in the disaster-affected population, but additional technical support is usually needed for adapting skills to the emergency, or introducing new techniques.

8.2.2 Phased approach

First of all, try to ensure that immediate needs are met. Even before any equipment or specialist staff can be brought in to set up water-treatment and distribution systems, there are many things that can be done to improve the quality of water available to the population, and a certain amount that can be done to increase the quantity available.

Priority actions
The fundamental rules to follow are these (adapted from Davis and Lambert, 1995).

Ensure sufficient quantity: at least 5 lcd, more if epidemics are present or threatening. Increase water availability to 15 lcd as soon as possible
- Bring in water by tanker if necessary.
- Develop well and spring sources to improve yield.
- Install overnight collection tanks for low-yielding springs.
- Improve access to existing supplies by means of footbridges, for example.

Protect water sources
- Organise defecation areas to keep human excreta separate from water sources.
- Organise use of streams and rivers to reduce contamination of drinking water.
- Control access to water sources: if possible, take the water to the people and prevent people from going to the water.
- Build simple protection for wells and springs.

Treat water, if necessary
- Chlorinate water in tanks and then distribute it, using whatever equipment is available, such as existing tanks, old tankers, bladder tanks.
- If this is not possible, do bucket chlorination (see section 8.4.2).
- Improve water source or install pre-treatment system to improve raw-water quality.

Ensure that adequate containers are available for collecting and storing water
- Each family should have containers with a capacity of at least 40 litres.

Ensure that soap is available
- Each family should have the equivalent of 250g of soap per person per month.

Rapid-reaction equipment
Lightweight, rapid-reaction water equipment has been used for several years by a number of agencies in acute emergencies. This includes bladder tanks (pillow tanks) and onion tanks, flexible pipework, lightweight pumps, and lightweight tap-stands. This equipment is easy to transport, quick and simple to use, and may be installed, used, packed up, and moved elsewhere easily if the population moves on. It allows the possibility of a rapid response without a large capital investment in one particular site, and helps to provide

minimum water supplies for the period before more permanent and higher-capacity supplies are installed. On assessment visits it is often possible to carry some lightweight equipment which could be used to set up a simple pumping, chlorination, and distribution system.

Longer-term solutions

Before developing a more permanent system, there should be some decision about the future of the emergency settlement. The choice of site for this should depend very much on the availability of a suitable longer-term water supply. See Chapter 6 on site selection. Minimum standards for water supply should be reached as soon as possible. If a central water treatment/storage installation is being set up or repaired, concentrate on making that operational and producing water within reasonable reach of people, rather than spreading resources to establish a distribution system too. Ensure that there is enough water available for increased consumption and a larger population at a later stage. See section 8.3 on water sources. As more equipment and other resources become available on site, start to develop the distribution system, using health information and mapping to prioritise areas to develop. If necessary, use water tankers to full gaps or supply large centres like hospitals and cholera-treatment centres. Use the following targets as a general guide for planning and implementing a water supply in an emergency settlement:

Within 2 weeks to 1 month: 5 lcd, within 1 km of shelters
Within 1 month to 3 months: 15 lcd, within 1 km of shelters
Within 3 to 6 months: 15 lcd or *ad lib*, within 500 m of shelters.

After three to six months, when the emergency period should have passed, the major priorities for water-supply programmes are operations and maintenance, reducing dependence on outside support, and preparing for the longer-term outcome of the situation.

8.2.3 Involving the disaster-affected community

During the development of the water-supply system, it is important to inform the users of plans and progress, through camp meetings or community-based activities (such as religious gatherings), information at water points, community-based workers, and water committees. Water committees and hygiene-promotion networks are very effective means of making contact with water-supply users and should be established early on in the programme. Their role may be quite broad, but their basic function should be to represent the views and problems of water users to the implementing agency, to help to channel information and ideas from the agency to the users, and to help to manage participation in the installation and management of water supplies, particularly at the tap or hand-pump end of the system.

Information should be gathered in order to plan where taps should be sited, what is the best design for washing facilities, what would be the best way to deal with waste water, etc.

Hygiene information should be provided, if needed, to the disaster-affected people, to help them make best use of what may be limited water supplies, in an environment where hygienic practices are not easy to observe.

Agencies recruiting from within the disaster-affected community need to make people aware what staff they need. If they particularly want to recruit women, this needs to be made clear and communicated effectively.

8.2.4 Links with other sectors

During the planning and implementation of water supplies, use information from health staff to help you to decide on priorities for system development, such as where to go next with the distribution network, or reacting to water-quality problems. Co-ordinate with staff in other sectors to plan supplies to facilities such as health centres and orphanages, and possible supplies to public toilets. Get feedback on drainage problems, breakdowns, and breakages. Stay in touch with camp managers for information on possible population movements, security problems, and political developments.

8.3 Water sources

8.3.1 Introduction

In most cases, particularly where a large population is involved, there is very little choice of water source. For large populations, at least in the short term, what is usually needed is a source of surface water that can be treated by using techniques and equipment that are tried, tested, and available, to produce sufficient water of adequate quality. Consider the following important points when choosing a water source.

Water quantity and reliability
There should be enough water to supply long-term requirements throughout the year, unless it is planned to supplement it at times by tankering. Where water is drawn from controlled supplies such as irrigation canals, arrangements should be made to avoid water being cut off at critical times.

Water quality
It should be possible to supply raw water without treatment, or the water should be treatable using available techniques and equipment. Its qualities that are difficult to change by treatment, such as salinity, should be within acceptable limits.

The four most important measurements of raw-water quality when choosing a water source are as follows:

- **Turbidity** (cloudiness), which will determine the type and level of treatment needed. This is measured in Turbidity Units, or NTU. See section 8.4.2 for recommended turbidity limits.

- **pH** (degree of acidity or alkalinity), which should be in the range 6.5 to 8.5 (according to WHO).

- **Faecal contamination**, in the case of water which is normally not intended for disinfection before consumption, such as spring water in a small settlement. See the Sphere Project *Minimum Standards* document.

- **Saltiness**, usually measured by electrical conductivity, which should be less than 2,000 uS/cm. This measurement is used to calculate Total Dissolved Solids (TDS) (which should be less than 1,000 mg/l for human consumption), and is primarily an indication of palatability and possible contamination. A simple taste test is often more useful than measuring conductivity for determining palatability, and should certainly be carried out in any case.

These tests can be carried out using simple apparatus. Many other physical and chemical properties can be measured in the field, using portable, simple, and inexpensive equipment; but the tests mentioned above are the core tests which provide information to decide whether or not to use a water source, whether or not to treat the water, and what sort of treatment might be necessary.

As well as measurements of water quality, a sanitary survey can reveal a lot about likely sources of contamination, and for biological water quality is far more indicative of long-term water quality and possible solutions than is a test for faecal contamination. See also section 8.10.3.

8.3.2 Surface water

Introduction
Surface water in lakes, rivers, and streams can easily be seen, measured, and sampled for testing. It is usually possible to learn a lot about its history, its behaviour, who it belongs to, where it comes from, and where it goes. Surface water is available for use immediately. But surface water is also of dubious and variable quality — it should always be assumed to be contaminated — and the quantity available may vary a great deal too.

Assessing surface-water quantity
You may be able to obtain information on the availability of surface water from hydrological data, reports, and local information before going to the site. Local people may be able to give reliable information about seasonal water availability. But often the only way to be sure how much water is available is by direct measurement. Large lakes, rivers, and streams may not need to be measured, as long as they are there all the year round and do not disappear in the dry season. Small streams and springs should be measured with a bucket

or a measuring weir to ensure that they have enough water to supply what is needed. It is necessary to investigate the usual variations in flow during the year. In a long-term project, measurements would normally be made every month or so for at least one year. In an emergency, one may have to rely on local information about stream and spring flows. Open wells may be pump-tested to measure their yield.

8.3.3 Protecting surface-water sources

A lot can be done to improve raw-water quality, and to make any treatment more effective and simple by improving the protection of surface-water sources. Options include pumping water from the source to a more distant point to avoid contamination by users; using physical protection such as a jetty on a lake to enable people to collect water without stepping in it; organising activities that take place in the water, such as laundry and bathing, in such a way as to avoid contamination upstream of the intake or the point of collection; and siting and building intakes in such a way that the raw water taken is of the highest quality possible to start with. The Pumping Manual supplied with the Oxfam Water Pumping Pack gives more details of simple source-protection techniques.

8.3.4 Ground-water

Introduction
Ground-water cannot be seen or measured directly. Unless there are ground-water supplies already developed and in use at or near the site, there is no direct way to judge how much water, if any, is available, for how long, and of what quality it is. It usually takes too long for it to be assessed, reached, and developed for it to be of use in the first phase of most emergency situations. On the other hand, it is usually of very good biological quality and only very rarely needs any treatment, other than chlorination. Where emergency water supplies are based on ground-water, the wells left behind when the disaster-affected community leaves may provide a long-term benefit for local people, and wells are a very appropriate water source for small groups of people.

Ground-water investigation
Information may be available from the following sources:

Existing information: previous records, or existing boreholes nearby. These may give information on likely yield and some indication of likely water quality.

Ground-water surveys: a ground-water specialist may do a survey on site, often using electrical resistivity equipment, to build up a picture of underground conditions and to interpret this information to give an indication of the presence of water and likely quantities. This information may be supported by a desk study.

Test or production drilling: very little can be said definitively about ground-water until it has been physically reached by drilling or digging and has been extracted. Test drilling with small-diameter boreholes, or even full-size production boreholes, may be the only way to find out if there is adequate water available, if it is possible to reach it and to extract it, and if it is of suitable quality.

The most important parameters to be measured are **yield, pH, conductivity,** and **dissolved iron**. If ground-water is to be used for long periods of time, the presence of trace elements such as arsenic and fluoride should also be checked.

8.3.5 Options for reaching ground-water

Drilling
Water-well drilling is a specialised activity that needs full-time experienced management in order to avoid spending large amounts of money for little or no result. There is a range of equipment available, from very large to relatively small rotary drilling machines to percussion (cable tool) rigs, which are much slower in hard rock, but cheaper and simpler to operate. The options to consider, if it is decided to go ahead with a drilling project, are whether to do the drilling directly or to employ a contractor to do it. If a contractor is hired, a comprehensive drilling contract will be needed to ensure that the maximum number of productive wells is drilled for the money spent. If direct implementation is chosen, it may be possible to hire a drilling rig and operate it, or to buy a lightweight rig. This last option would normally be taken only if there were no suitable contractors able to take their own equipment to work in the location, or if there was no suitable equipment available to hire. To buy, operate, and maintain even a small drilling rig involves a large investment in the purchase of the equipment and recruitment and training of staff. However, if this option is chosen, there are several models of small and relatively cheap rig available. Oxfam stocks a rotary rig with a range of equipment capable of drilling wells of 100 to 150mm diameter and up to 100m deep, in geological formations ranging from soft sands through to hard rocks.

Hand-drilled and jetted wells
In clays, sands, and fine gravels, wells may be drilled or jetted by hand up to 30 or 40 metres deep and up to 200 mm in diameter, yielding enough water for a handpump. The techniques and equipment used are relatively cheap and simple, and progress is much faster than with hand-dug wells.

Well digging
Wells have been dug for many centuries in different parts of the world, using simple techniques that have been developed in recent years to improve safety and speed. Wells may be dug in a variety of geological formations; in hard rock, progress is slow, and specialist techniques like rock blasting or power-tool digging are needed. Hand-dug wells are rarely more than 30 metres deep. Where the water table is deeper than this, another option should be sought,

unless there is local experience of deeper wells than this. The capital equipment needed for well digging is relatively cheap and portable, and the techniques used are fairly easy to understand. Although a well-digging programme can be relatively quick to get started, the time it takes to dig each well makes this an unsuitable technique for most acute emergencies. One well, supplying from 300 to 1,000 people, may take weeks or even months to complete, depending on the water-table depth and geological conditions. However, hand-dug wells have been successfully used to provide longer-term supplies in refugee camps, for example in several of the Mozambican camps in Malawi. Oxfam holds a range of well-digging equipment in stock, including survey augers, well-ring moulds, tripods, compressors, and de-watering pumps.

8.3.6 Ground-water monitoring

Ground-water is not an infinite resource. The water pumped from a well may come from an isolated and irreplaceable aquifer, or one that is replenished at a very limited rate. It is important, where there is any doubt about the capacity of the aquifer to supply the necessary amount of water over the long term, to monitor ground-water behaviour. This may need advice from a hydro-geologist to set up the monitoring system and interpret results; but even without specialist advice, a simple system can be used to measure the static water level in a number of sample wells and to plot changes in the level of the water table. If there is a long-term drop in the water table, abstraction rates may need to be reduced to a more sustainable level, and alternative water sources may need to be sought. Monitor electrical conductivity too, in case the quality of the ground-water changes, particularly in coastal areas where salt-water intrusion is a possibility. Check with the local water Ministry before starting a drilling programme, for information on local ground-water resource problems and for information about controls on drilling and ground-water abstraction that may apply. Ground-water is an important and scarce resource in many countries.

8.4 Water treatment

8.4.1 Purpose of treatment

The major purpose of water treatment is to remove and/or destroy disease-causing organisms (pathogens) in the water. Disinfection with chlorine is often done in emergencies, to destroy micro-organisms and to provide an extra level of protection by leaving some disinfecting power in the water. In turbid waters many of the pathogens are closely associated with the suspended solids, which have to be removed by settling or filtration before the water can be effectively disinfected. This is the case for most surface waters, which are the most common water source used in large-scale emergencies. The water should also have a taste, odour, and appearance which people find acceptable, so that they do not go to drink from unsafe sources instead.

8.4.2 Water-treatment options

Introduction

The treatment techniques used in emergencies should be reliable and tolerant of variable standards of operation, able to cope with a range of raw-water qualities, easy to measure and monitor, using resources and skills which are readily available, and cheap and effective.

The techniques generally used by Oxfam in emergencies are flocculation with aluminium sulphate (alum) and sedimentation in tanks, where necessary, and chlorination with High Test Hypochlorite (HTH) chlorine powder. Other chemicals may be used for both flocculation and disinfection. (These are described in Oxfam's internal Guidelines for Water Treatment in Emergencies.)

Water intakes

The point at which water is taken from a lake or river, the intake, may be designed, located, and built to ensure that the highest possible quality of water is abstracted for treatment. See section 8.3.3 above.

Pre-treatment

The raw water may be passed through a pre-treatment filter or roughing filter, to remove some of the suspended solids before going on to further treatment processes described below. This makes these subsequent treatments more rapid, effective, and cheaper to achieve. Oxfam is developing standard equipment for installing roughing filters to reduce turbidity by 90–95 per cent over the turbidity range of 50–500 NTU. These take some time to install and are not generally suitable for the first phase of emergencies.

Coagulation and flocculation

In emergencies, alum is the most commonly used chemical for coagulation (chemical dosing to encourage small particles in turbid water to agglomerate). It works best in the pH range 6.0 to 7.5, and pH adjustment with an acid or an alkali may be needed for waters outside this range. Ferric salts, which are effective over a wider pH range, are also used by some agencies but are generally less widely available. Jar tests are done with a sample of the water to be treated, to determine how much alum is to be added. The aim is to reduce the turbidity to less than 5 NTU for chlorination. Oxfam stocks a kit for determining the correct dose to use and for checking turbidity. During operations, the alum is dissolved in water and the solution added to raw water as it enters the tank, for rapid mixing. A swirling motion set up by water entering the tank at an angle provides conditions for gentle mixing and flocculation (where agglomerations of small particles come together to form large collections of solids, or flocs). When the tank is full and the water stills, then the flocs formed can settle out with the suspended solids. This normally takes between three and six hours. The clear water can be drawn off, leaving the sediment in the bottom of the tank. The sediment has to be emptied and the tank cleaned from time to time. The daily operations should be recorded to monitor the quantity of alum used and the turbidity of the raw and treated water, to ensure that the correct dose is always used, and to refine the treatment technique. For health and safety reasons, the dosage rate needs to be adjusted according to variations in raw-water quality, and care should be taken to avoid excessive aluminium being carried over into the water consumed.

Disinfection
Although pre-treatment and sedimentation can remove many of the pathogens associated with suspended solids in water, many remain and should be killed before the water is fit to consume. Although there are a number of different options for disinfection, including boiling, ultraviolet-light treatment, and several different chemical methods, the most common method for emergency work is chlorination, because it has the following features:

- It destroys pathogens present in the water within an acceptable time. (Note that some species of helminth cysts and protozoa are resistant to chlorine. The best way to deal with them is to improve protection of the water source.)
- It can perform within the range of temperatures and physical conditions encountered.
- It disinfects without leaving any effects harmful to humans.
- It permits simple and quick measurement of strength and concentration in water.
- It leaves sufficient active residual concentration as a safeguard against post-treatment contamination.
- It is readily and reliably available at reasonable cost.
- It can be transported, stored, and handled safely and with few special precautions.

Boiling water is rarely a practical option, particularly in emergencies, and the environmental costs may be great.

Water should have less than 5 NTU of turbidity for chlorination to be most effective. If the water contains a lot of suspended or dissolved solids, the chlorine demand (the amount of chlorine to be added before a disinfecting concentration is produced) will be greater, and the dosage is unlikely to be totally effective. The chlorine demand is determined by adding different volumes of chlorine solution to samples of the water to be treated and measuring the residual chlorine level. (Oxfam's internal Guidelines for Water Treatment in Emergencies give more detail.) In extreme circumstances, even very turbid water may be chlorinated, though the treatment is of very limited effect, and the taste produced by adding the necessary amount of chlorine needed to meet the chlorine demand would probably be unacceptable to most people.

Sufficient chlorine should be added to give a free residual chlorine concentration of 0.2 to 0.5 mg/litre (ppm) after half an hour in the water. This is sufficient to kill all susceptible pathogens and to provide disinfecting power in the water, in case of contamination in the distribution system or after collection. The correct dose of chlorine may be estimated by adding a range of quantities of 1 per cent chlorine solution to samples of water and testing the free chlorine residual after 30 minutes of contact time. The water should be tasted before distribution, to ensure that it is palatable.

For the treatment process, a 1 per cent chlorine solution is normally made up, and this solution is added to the treatment tanks as they fill up, to mix it well with the water. The water should be left for a contact time of half an hour after the addition and mixing of chlorine, for all pathogens to be killed before distribution. Chlorine works more rapidly at higher temperatures and at lower pH. If the pH is above 8.5, its disinfecting power is greatly reduced, and the contact time before distribution should be increased. If the pH exceeds 9, the water may need to be acidified with hydrochloric acid to make chlorination effective.

For bucket chlorination, after estimating the correct chlorine dose for the water to be chlorinated, staff should be positioned at water points or on routes between surface-water sources and their shelters, to add an appropriate quantity of 1 per cent chlorine solution, usually with a syringe. Staff will need guidance on adding the correct quantity to different sizes of water container.

There are some doubts about the long-term health effects of drinking chlorinated water. Most of the concern is about by-products of chlorination in waters with a high organic-compound content. In terms of public health, however, the risk of disease posed by not chlorinating water is very much greater than the risk from long-term consumption.

Whatever system is used, chlorination should be monitored daily, or more often if necessary, to check that the right dosage is used; the results should be recorded in a notebook or on a form, to enable problems to be traced.

Slow sand filtration
Slow sand filtration relies on the biological activity produced at the surface of a sand layer under water to remove nearly all pathogens. Slow sand filters can be operated in a range of temperatures. Once they are set up, they are very simple to operate and maintain, needing no chemical inputs.

The main disadvantage of slow sand filters is that the filtration rate is slow ($0.2m^3/m^2$/hour). Thus for a population of 10,000 people consuming 15 lcd, a filter area of $150m^2$ would be needed, assuming operation 12 hours per day, plus provision for cleaning filters. Building filters of this type takes time and space, which are often limited in emergencies. It is a useful technique for more stable phases. Oxfam stocks equipment and guidelines for setting up slow sand filters, using standard Oxfam tanks.

8.4.3 Phased approach

At the beginning of the emergency response, when supplying a population with water from a turbid water source, the quickest solution is normally to do some temporary work to install an improved intake from the water source, to pump the water to tanks for flocculation and sedimentation with alum, to chlorinate in separate tanks, and then to distribute the water. At this stage the system would be operated for up to 24 hours per day, to get the most out of the equipment available.

After some weeks, the system could be expanded by adding tanks and pumps in parallel with the first ones, to increase the output of the system while reducing the operating hours.

After some months, longer-term lower-input solutions may be sought, to reduce dependency on imported chemicals and cut operating costs. This might involve replacing the coagulation and flocculation process with roughing filtration and slow sand filtration, using the same tanks. Some rearrangement of tanks would be needed, and space would have to be left for this from the beginning of the construction. This should be planned for and a budget allowed from an early stage in the project.

8.4.4 Packaged water-treatment systems

It is possible to buy packaged water-treatment systems: self-contained mobile units that take in raw water and produce high-quality drinking water. These are commonly used for field supplies to the military and for emergency supplies to hospitals. Most systems are unable to deal with high-turbidity raw water and are less easy to adapt to different situations than a set of independent components that can be combined in a number of ways. In general they are unable to produce the quantities of water needed to supply populations of more than a few thousand people; they are thus not suitable as the main water supply in large emergencies, though they can be used very successfully for supplying water to field hospitals, feeding centres, or way stations.

8.5 Water pumping

8.5.1 Applications

Pumps are needed to move water uphill and from place to place, for supplying raw water to treatment systems, for moving water around treatment systems, for water distribution, and for filling and discharging water tankers. For all of these functions, try to use water sources that can achieve this as far as possible by gravity. Keep the number of pumping stages to a minimum. Where water has to be pumped uphill to supply a settlement, aim to concentrate all of the pumping activity in the supply to the storage/treatment tanks, which should be located if possible to feed the distribution system by gravity. Pumps are also needed for lifting water out of boreholes and wells. In flat country with few surface-water sources, pumping will be unavoidable.

8.5.2 Choosing and installing pumps

Types of pump

For most emergencies involving surface-water sources, surface-mounted petrol or diesel-driven centrifugal pumps are used. Several agencies, including Oxfam, stock standard centrifugal pumps for a range of applications. For ground-water abstraction, multi-stage submersible electrical or mechanically driven helical rotor pumps are used, or handpumps based on a variety of pumping mechanisms.

Petrol-driven pumps are lightweight, cheap, and increasingly reliable, but are rarely used beyond the acute emergency stage, because of their long-term unreliability and cost. For long-term applications, diesel or electrically driven pumps are the most reliable and cheap. If sufficient high-voltage electrical power is available, electrical pumps may be a good choice, because they have very low maintenance requirements and are extremely reliable. For pumps with low power requirements, solar power is a possible long-term option. However, choosing and installing electrical pumps needs specialist advice and is rarely done in emergencies, except in the context of rehabilitating urban water supplies, or equipping boreholes with pre-specified submersible electrical pumps.

The most simple type of pump is a bucket and rope or windlass. Where a relatively small or scattered population is involved, with access to open wells, this may be the most appropriate form of pump to choose.

Oxfam stocks four sizes of standard surface-mounted centrifugal pump with spares packs for moving water over a range of heads and discharges, as well as progressive cavity and submersible electric pumps for ground-water.

Procuring pumps

Although it is often recommended that materials and equipment should be locally purchased, in the case of motor pumps this may not be the case. It is very important that the pump chosen should be well known and have a good record of service in the sorts of conditions faced. The source of spare parts should be reliable. Very often local supplies of spare parts are small and quickly exhausted by a large operation. Where the agency does not have an established relationship with a supplier, it may be more difficult to get a guarantee of spare-parts availability and back-up when things go wrong. Many suppliers are simply traders and have no specialist knowledge of pumps.

Sizing and installing diesel-driven surface-mounted centrifugal pumps *(More details in the Oxfam Water Pumping Pack Manual)*

- Use pump performance curves to select the correct size of pump or combination of pumps for the application required.
- Remember to de-rate pumps for altitude and temperature, and provide good ventilation and shelter to avoid high temperatures around the pump.
- Where very large flows are required, it is more prudent to install several small pumps rather than one very large one. Providing standby pumps will be cheaper when small pumps are used.
- Where large pumping heads are required, plan to achieve this with several stages of pumping. The Oxfam P3H pump has a maximum discharge head of 60m.
- If larger single lifts cannot be avoided, use higher-rated pipes near the bottom of the lift, and anchor pipe with thrust blocks to avoid damage by water hammer.
- Suction lifts should be less than 7m. Keep suction pipes as short and as straight as possible.
- Site intakes to avoid blockage of foot-valves and strainers, and ingress of sand and silt. Position inlets at least 0.3m below the water surface, to avoid vortices forming and allowing air to enter the suction hose.
- Avoid unnecessary tight bends and fittings in the delivery pipe, to reduce friction losses.
- Fix pumps firmly to the ground on a concrete slab or heavy timbers pegged to the ground. Secure inlet and outlet pipes close to the pump to avoid damage to connections through vibration.
- Position the pump to avoid oil and diesel contaminating the water source, particularly when shallow wells are used.

8.5.3 Pump operation and maintenance

Pumping is a critical operation, which demands careful selection and installation of equipment and then planned preventive maintenance, to avoid system failures and large unforeseen costs. Pump-operating staff need clear job descriptions and training to define their responsibilities. For instance, it is usual to limit pump operators' mechanical responsibility to oil and filter changes, if there are mechanics available to do major services and repairs. Unless the division of responsibility is made very clear, important maintenance work can be forgotten, or unqualified staff may attempt to make repairs and make the problem worse. Pump operators should be provided with a logbook for each pump, to record such details as operating hours and fuel consumption. This should be analysed every month, along with water-supply figures, to check that pumps are performing correctly and that fuel consumption is within acceptable limits. Pump operators should inform the mechanics when the next service is due and report any unusual noises or changes in pump performance. Mechanical problems such as impeller damage due to cavitation may be spotted by regular monitoring. Services, spare-parts use, and major mechanical problems should all be recorded for each pump, to keep track of how much is spent on each pump and help to decide when to replace pumps or look more closely at the operations and maintenance system. Spare parts should be stocked in the field, and supplies should be assured through head offices or locally.

8.6 Water tankering

8.6.1 Applications

Tankering can be used to move water from sources to a whole population to provide the main water supply, to fill gaps in distribution systems, to cover periods of drought or breakdown, or until alternative systems are installed. Tankers can often be mobilised almost immediately; if water tankers are not available, milk and fuel tankers may be used, or flat-bed trucks made into tankers by fitting specially designed bladder tanks or rigid tanks on the back.

However, tankering is an expensive and high-maintenance operation, which should generally be avoided if there is another option. The operation can be easily disrupted by security problems, strikes, and bad road conditions.

8.6.2 Tankering costs

An example of typical water-tankering costs is given below.

A settlement of 50,000 people requires 10 lcd in an emergency from a source 20km away on a dirt road. It takes half an hour to fill the tanker, half an hour for the trip each way, and half an hour to discharge. The operating day is ten hours long. An average of 4 trips per day is possible, allowing 20 per cent downtime for repairs and maintenance. Each tanker of 15,000l can supply 60,000 l per day, so 9 tankers would be needed.

Each tanker might have a depreciation cost of £1,000 per month and a fuel and maintenance cost of £2,000 per month, plus driver's salary of £1,000 per month. The total cost is £27,000 per month, or 15 pence per person served per day.

8.6.3 Tankering operations

Water-tankering operations need careful planning and management to ensure that reliable supplies are maintained and costs are kept down. The following points should be borne in mind.

- Choose the most reliable tankers and drivers available. An unreliable tanker and bad driver will soon cost more than they are worth.
- Monitor drivers' activities; there is a great temptation for drivers to sell water either inside or outside the settlement. This slows down the operation and means less water for the people who need it.
- Ensure that enough drivers are available to cover absence for sickness and breaks. Avoid overworking drivers.
- Keep a logbook for each tanker to record trips made, distance covered, breakdowns, etc.
- Provide a tank at the destination to allow the tanker to discharge rapidly. Do not allow water to be distributed straight from the tanker.
- Provide hard and well-drained surfaces at tanker filling and discharge points, and adequate space for tankers to queue and turn around.
- Provide pumps for filling and emptying tankers rapidly. The faster they can turn round, the better. Make it clear who is responsible for fuel and maintenance on pumps which are fitted to tankers.
- Chlorinate water in the tankers during filling, to allow contact during the journey. Monitor free chlorine residual during discharge.
- Where different capacities of tanker are being used, provide a measuring cup for chlorine powder for each size of tanker, or a chart of volume of chlorine compound for each tanker.
- Give drivers responsibility for ensuring that the water is correctly chlorinated and reporting problems to their supervisor.

8.7 Water storage

8.7.1 Storage capacity

Water storage is needed for treatment processes, for controlling the distribution of water, and for providing a stock of water in the camp in case of mechanical breakdown, lack of fuel, security problems, etc. and for routine maintenance, such as cleaning tanks or upgrading treatment systems. The amount of storage to build into the system depends on the likelihood of these various factors, as well as on the amount of storage needed for treatment and for overnight supply of raw water from gravity sources. As a rough guide, plan for 12–24 hours of storage in a centralised water-supply system, depending on the reliability of the supply. Thus for a settlement of 50,000 people, assuming 15 lcd, allow 375 to 750m³ of storage. Stored water should be distributed within a few hours of being chlorinated, or the chlorine residual may become too low to provide continued disinfection. When installing storage and treatment tanks, allow enough space for adding tanks later on if necessary. The storage capacity should be increased if the supply is unreliable. It is better to have increased storage capacity at a central level than for people to store large quantities of water in their homes.

Health centres should have their own storage tanks to ensure that they always have access to water, even if the general supply system fails for some time.

8.7.2 Storage tanks

There are many different types of storage tank available. The most rapid to install are flexible bladder or pillow tanks and onion tanks, both made of reinforced PVC. Onion tanks have the advantage of providing a relatively deep body of water, which is useful for coagulation and sedimentation. Both types of tank are available in sizes ranging from 2 to 30m^3. These tanks can easily be dismantled and taken elsewhere in unstable situations, but do not last for more than a few months, unless they are well protected from the weather and from wear and tear.

Oxfam-type tanks, made from bolt-together steel sheets, a butyl rubber liner, and a tarpaulin roof, are available in 10, 45, 70 and 95m^3 sizes. They are heavier than most other kit tanks, and take more time, preparation, and skill to erect, but they are robust and may last for five to ten years without major problems. They can also be adapted into filter systems at some stage.

Large tanks of the type used in the water industry may be built with steel or reinforced glass-fibre panels bolted together, but they need specialist and experienced staff to construct them correctly.

Tanks may be built on site using masonry, block or brickwork, reinforced concrete, or ferro-cement. This takes more time than putting together tank kits. For tanks with a capacity of more than 5m^3, careful design and construction are needed to ensure that they hold water and are not potentially dangerous.

For storing very large quantities of raw water and as part of the treatment process, earth dams may be built. This requires specialist engineering skills and a very large number of workers, or access to earth-moving equipment, and may take months to complete. Temporary dams to facilitate water abstraction may be built rapidly with stone, timber, and plastic sheeting.

In desperate circumstances, temporary tanks may be constructed with holes in the ground, or earth bunds, or timber and plastic sheeting. It is difficult to make such tanks water-tight and to build in outlets.

8.8 Water distribution

8.8.1 System design and installation

Once water has been treated, it has to be put within easy reach of the users, otherwise they will not be able to collect enough of it. Aim for a water point within 500 metres of each shelter. The position of water points will depend primarily on the topographical and engineering constraints, but should also respect the advice of the users, whose views should be sought during planning and implementation The distribution system should be planned to allow for expansion of the camp and for increased water consumption, to avoid having to replace or double up pipes at a later stage. Aim to produce a system layout that gives about 0.125 litres/second (7.5 litres/minute) at each tap. The manual supplied with the Oxfam Water Distribution Pack provides more details and a worked example.

Where possible, use the slope of the ground to achieve gravity flow with sufficient head at each tap-stand. Lay pipes as close as possible to a continuous slope. In very hilly areas it may be necessary to install air vents to prevent air locks at high points, or to site tap-stands to act as venting points. If there is a height difference of much more than 40m between the tank outlet and the lowest taps, a pressure-relief valve or a break-pressure tank may be needed. Where the ground is very flat, it may be necessary to build up a platform for a storage tank, or to install a pump in the distribution system. The minimum water level in the tank should be at least 2 metres above the tap. A simple branched distribution main is often used, because it provides the best access to the water points for the length of pipe used. The 32mm branch pipes should not be more than 10m long, unless there is a lot of head available, to keep friction losses to a minimum. Alternatively, a ring main may be installed, as this allows flow in both directions, so all taps can be served, even when part of the main is closed or blocked. In large camps or in urban situations, quite complex systems are developed, particularly where the systems have to grow to cope with an expanding population.

Do not rely on other agencies to tell you in advance where they are planning to build health centres and other places that will need to be connected to the distribution system. It is usually necessary to visit them and find out their plans, to warn them if their preferred sites are difficult to reach with the distribution system. Make sure that all the agencies are aware of the plans for the water system. It may be necessary to supply additional storage for some centres in case of water shortage. The agency concerned should take responsibility for this storage inside their facilities and for the quality of the water stored. This may mean that they have to re-chlorinate water stored over a long time to provide an acceptable level of chlorine residual, and they may need advice and training on this.

8.8.2 Phased implementation

As with all other aspects of water-system implementation, the complete system cannot be built overnight, and engineers should design to meet immediate needs in a way that can be built upon to produce the final system layout.

In Benaco camp, Tanzania in 1994, the water supply for 200,000 Rwandan refugees was begun by chlorinating water from a reservoir in bladder tanks and distributing via 10 tap-stands of 6 taps, in order to improve water quality and avoid people going into the reservoir to collect water. At the same time, work started on laying pipes for the main distribution system from the treatment works, also under construction. As the pipes were laid, gate valves were installed in front of each ferrule strap where branches were made for tap-stands, so that water could be supplied as far as possible as the work progressed. To save time, a small number of large tap-stand groups was installed. At Musahwa Hill, where there was more time, smaller and more scattered tap-stand groups were installed, and this was better for the users.

8.8.3 Distribution equipment

Standard equipment
It is important that distribution equipment used in emergencies is quick and easy to use, robust, and compatible with equipment from other agencies and with standard water fittings. Oxfam uses a range of distribution mains, fittings, and tap-stands which may be combined in different ways with tanks and pumps to install a distribution system suitable for most conditions that are likely to be encountered.

Pipe
In acute emergencies, flexible hose, either reinforced plastic, or textile-based fire hose (lay-flat hose) may be used, commonly not buried. This may be transported easily and set up very quickly, but will not last for more than a few months at most. For more permanent systems, either uPVC or polyethylene (PE) pipe is used. uPVC pipe is cheaper to buy and much cheaper to air-freight than coils of PE pipe, can usually be purchased locally and can be assembled quickly, using the couplings which are an integral part of the pipe. However, uPVC pipe needs to be buried for protection and stability. PE pipe, which comes in coils or straight lengths, is more expensive and needs to be joined, using special compression couplings, electrofusion couplings, or butt welding. During early phases of an emergency, coils of PE pipe can be used to install distribution main very quickly, using compression couplings every 100 metres, with no need to bury the pipe straight away. Where ground conditions do not allow pipe to be buried, PE pipe may be laid on the surface, as it is much less brittle than uPVC pipe and less prone to degradation by exposure to ultraviolet light.

Oxfam generally uses only 3" pipe for distribution mains, and 4" or 6" where larger populations are to be served.

Taps

Distribution in large-scale emergency water systems is usually via tap-stands, each with several taps. Oxfam uses a self-closing design of tap called the Taflo valve. The tap-stands are connected to the distribution mains using self-tapping ferrule straps and 32mm PE pipe.

Other fittings

Where the system is to be used for a long time, bulk water meters on tank outlets are useful for measuring water supplied. Pressure-reducing valves, check valves, and float valves may all be needed to assist in the operation of the system.

8.9 Water collection and use

8.9.1 Introduction

Water supply does not stop when clean water reaches taps. Unless the taps themselves and people's facilities for using the water are well designed, installed, and maintained, only half of the job has been done, and full benefits for health are unlikely to be achieved.

The first point of contact between the water users and the water system is the taps. Unless people have containers to collect and store water, consumption will be low and they will have no control over their access to water when it is needed. Well-designed water containers enable people to collect, store, and use water without contaminating it. People need a place to wash clothes and to bathe in privacy, to be able to live hygienically in crowded conditions. Particularly for washing clothes, it is far easier to go to the water point than to carry the water to another place; this is of great concern to women, if it is they who carry most of the family's water. Men may not see this as a particular problem, because they might be less aware of the work involved. If some sort of laundry facility is not provided near a water source, people tend to wash their clothes on any convenient hard surface nearby. This can cause problems of uncontrolled drainage, and in many camps there simply are not suitable places to wash clothes. Washing facilities are perhaps not a high priority early in an emergency, compared with other aspects of water supply and sanitation. In Kibumba Rwandan refugee camp in Goma, from 1994 to 1996 there were no improved public washing facilities because of a shortage of water. The health statistics do not suggest that conditions there were worse than in the other three camps nearby, where washing facilities were installed. However, washing facilities are important for personal and social reasons as well as for health.

8.9.2 Design and installation

Consulting users
Try to consult people on the following points:

- Where would consumers prefer taps to be placed? If they are wrongly placed, people living close to the tap-stands may intimidate other water users. Ensure that poor and marginalised groups have access to the taps.
- If the taps can be used only at certain times of the day because of water-supply restrictions, what hours would the users prefer?
- What size of water container is most appropriate for people collecting water? If children are collecting, they may prefer a 5-litre or a 10-litre container rather than a larger one.
- Should some of the taps be specially designed to be easier for children or older people to use? For example, there might be a smaller distance between tap and base for smaller water containers.
- Ensure that tap-stands, showers, and washbasins can be used easily by pregnant women, the elderly, sick people, and children. Ask some of these people to test the first installations.
- Are taps and washing facilities sited to avoid security problems, particularly for women?
- Does the siting of taps and washing areas correspond to administrative or community groupings within the camp?

Laundry facilities
Washing slabs should be provided close to the water-collection points, but sited to avoid waste-water problems around the taps. It may be convenient to build them alongside the drainage channels from tap-stands and use the same disposal method. Aim to provide one washing slab or basin per 100 people. The design chosen should depend on the preference of the users. Some people prefer to stand while washing clothes; others prefer to kneel. It is better to provide a slab with some sort of basin, as many people may not have their own basins for soaking and washing clothes. Wash-basins should be large enough to wash blankets in.

Personal washing facilities
It is more difficult to give guidelines for the number of showers to provide, as many people may prefer to wash where they sleep, even if it means carrying water home. Use a target of one shower cubicle per 500 people as a rough guide, but find out what practices and preferences should be taken into account in each situation. Shower blocks for men and for women should be separate structures, particularly if plastic sheeting is used for construction, as this quickly tends to get holes in it. Shower cubicles should have a hard and cleanable floor, usually stone, brick, or concrete with a smooth mortar finish, and walls to provide privacy. Water is usually carried into the showers by bucket. In the long term it is better to build showers from local materials such

as thatching grass or dry stone masonry, which can be maintained and repaired by the users and is less likely to be stolen.

In cold climates, showers should be provided inside buildings. The water may need to be piped to the shower and may need to be heated.

Water containers
Each family should have containers for collecting and storing water with a total capacity of at least 40 litres. The containers should have a small opening for filling, with a tight-fitting cap (usually the cap goes missing and is replaced with a cork made of local materials). Buckets should have a tight-fitting lid with an opening for pouring. They should be small enough to be carried easily by adults (normally no more than 20 litres), and some small containers should be provided for children. The containers should be light, hard-wearing, and made of plastic or sheet metal. Many thousands of containers may need to be air-freighted in an emergency, so containers that stack to save cargo space have a great advantage. Oxfam has developed a stackable jerrican, essentially a bucket with a permanent snap-on lid and a covered filling and pouring spout. In long-term situations local production of sheet-metal containers may be established, and it is usually possible to buy jerricans and buckets on the local market.

8.9.3 Soap

Soap is an important aid to personal and domestic hygiene. It should be available to people affected by disasters, to enable them to reduce their exposure to hygiene-related disease. Ashes or mud can also be effective for hand-washing, but a preference for soap is more or less universal, and it does encourage personal hygiene and the washing of clothes, with a demonstrated impact on health. A supply of the equivalent of 250g per person per month should be made available to the disaster-affected population. Soap should be used in preference to detergents, which cause more blockages in waste-water disposal systems.

8.9.4 Drainage of water points

Waste water from water-collection points and water-use facilities is a low-level direct risk to health, as it may contain faecal contamination from dirty bodies and clothes, and may cause secondary problems as a breeding site for disease vectors such as flies and mosquitoes. See Chapter 12 for guidance on disposing of waste water.

8.9.5 Maintenance and repair

For successful management of water points and facilities, the users should be involved. It helps enormously if the water points are relatively small and scattered, so that people can more easily identify them as their own. Link this with community zones (easier to do in planned camps). A water committee should be set up during the design and construction stage to ensure that users' views are heard and to establish responsibility for careful use and maintenance of the facilities. When construction is finished, hand over the facilities to the water committees and make sure that it is clear who is responsible for what: what the agency is to provide (spare parts for taps, etc.), and what the users are to provide (labour and local materials for repairs, etc.).

8.10 Water testing

8.10.1 Why test water?

Water is tested for the following reasons:

- For choosing water sources. Tests are done to see if the water can be drunk without treatment, or to determine what treatment methods are needed. See section 8.3.2
- For monitoring water quality once supplies are established; monitoring the quality of untreated water; and monitoring the performance of the treatment system.
- For monitoring water quality at the point of consumption, to see whether it has become contaminated during collection and storage.

8.10.2 Routine water-quality testing

Monitoring the quality of water supplied
Once the water source has been chosen and the treatment system established, they should be monitored regularly to check that safe water is being supplied. If the treatment system succeeds consistently in producing water of less then 5 NTU turbidity and with a minimum residual free chlorine level of 0.2 mg/litre after a half-hour contact time, it can be assumed to be biologically safe. There is no need to do regular biological testing where a centrally managed water-treatment system including chlorination is operated, unless system monitoring shows that there are problems with the treatment process.

At a central water-treatment works, residual free chlorine should be checked every day, and also turbidity where treatment involves clarifying the water. During the early days of operating the system, this monitoring will need to be more frequent until the system is fine-tuned. If the raw-water quality is very variable, tests may need to be done after each rainfall or even on each tankful of water before distribution, but this is expensive and time-consuming to sustain in the long term. Generally, once the system operations are well established and the operators are familiar with the normal variations in raw-water quality, less frequent checks should be necessary. Simple forms or exercise books should be used to record information, including the operators responsible for the particular shift, to help to identify causes of problems found, and to allow long-term trends to be identified.

Where water is not treated and water quality depends on good protection of the source, biological testing is more important and should be established as a routine. The frequency of testing depends on the number of people using the source. Typically, a spring supplying a settlement of 5,000 people should be tested for faecal contamination every month.

Testing stored water
Once water is collected and stored in people's shelters, there are many possibilities of contamination, particularly if the water is stored for a long time, in open and metal containers. Testing biological quality is useful for gathering information on water storage and use, and for informing hygiene-promotion work or arguing for distribution of more or better water containers. Measurements of the residual free chlorine level in water after collection may be taken where recontamination is a concern.

8.10.3 Microbiological testing and sanitary surveys

Principle of microbiological testing
The principle of the most common microbiological water test is to isolate and count the number of *Escherichia coli* bacteria in the water sample. *E. coli* or faecal coliforms are present in mammal excreta, and their presence indicates faecal contamination, though not necessarily from human sources. There are two principal ways of doing the test: one is by the 'most probable number' (MPN) technique, and the other is by membrane filtration. The MPN technique needs to be performed in laboratory conditions, though it uses cheap and simple equipment; whereas membrane filtration can be done with portable equipment in the field, though reliable equipment is expensive to purchase and supply with consumable items. Samples are taken, tested within six hours, then incubated for 14 to 18 hours before the numbers of faecal coliforms can be estimated. Results are expressed as numbers of faecal coliforms per 100ml.

Oxfam uses a portable water-testing kit, which includes tests for the presence of faecal coliforms, indicators of faecal contamination. Other tests, for instance to identify cholera in water, require more specific techniques and are generally outside the scope of normal procedures.

Applications and limitations
Biological water-quality tests are a very useful means to obtain quantifiable data on the quality of water at a certain time. The results can be expressed simply and clearly to explain the situation to other people, and to allow comparisons to be made over time and between different places. But it is important to remember that tests on a single sample of water show its quality at the moment of collecting the sample only: they say nothing about the source of contamination or its duration. Biological testing should be carried out in

conjunction with a sanitary survey and the results should be interpreted together, to avoid drawing incorrect conclusions and possibly closing down sources unnecessarily, or ignoring serious risks of contamination which have not yet affected the source.

Sanitary surveys

A sanitary survey is a methodical assessment and description of a water source, which identifies possible sources of contamination and suggests remedial action. The survey is done with a prepared form, which helps the surveyor to check all the important features of the water source and record the information for interpretation, reporting, and comparison. While biological testing needs specialised equipment and skills, a sanitary survey can be carried out by anyone with some basic training and no special equipment. A sanitary survey should be carried out once every month on water supplies such as springs and wells which provide untreated water, and on piped water systems to check for leaks from pipes and valves and to check the free chlorine residual at the taps.

8.10.4 Responsibility for water testing

While responsibility for selecting water sources lies usually with the implementing agency, routine testing may be done by the agency responsible for health, by a health ministry, or by the water ministry. Where several different agencies are responsible for water supply, it can be useful for water testing to be done centrally (apart from the daily monitoring of treatment operations), and the results reported back to the agencies concerned.

Further reading

J. Davis and R. Lambert (1996) *Engineering in Emergencies: A practical guide for relief workers,* Chapters 9, 10, 11, and 12, London: RedR/IT Publications

S. House and R. Reed (1997) *Emergency Water Sources: Guidelines for selection and treatment,* Loughborough University: Water, Engineering, and Development Centre (WEDC)

Oxfam (1997) Oxfam Guidelines for Water Treatment in Emergencies, unpublished internal document (not for general circulation), Oxford: Oxfam GB

Sphere Project (1999, forthcoming) *Humanitarian Charter and Minimum Standards in Disaster Response,* Chapter 2 section 3: 'Water Supply', published in Geneva by the Standing Committee for Humanitarian Response (SCHR) and Interaction. E-mail: sphere@ifrc.org; internet: *www.sphereproject.org*

UNHCR (1992) *Water Manual for Refugee Situations*, Geneva: Programme Technical Support Section, UNHCR

WHO (1984) *Guidelines for Drinking Water Quality*, Vol. I: Recommendations, Geneva: WHO

WHO (1984) *Guidelines for Drinking Water Quality*, Vol. III: Drinking Water Quality Control in Small Community Supplies, Geneva: WHO

9 | Excreta disposal

9.1 Introduction

The primary barrier to transmission of excreta-related disease, whatever the transmission route, is the containment and safe disposal of human excreta. All other measures, such as improved personal hygiene and water treatment, are secondary to this. Therefore, excreta disposal should be tackled as one of the small number of first-priority interventions from the start of any emergency response. It is very important also for supporting the dignity and morale of people affected by disasters to provide decent facilities for defecation as quickly as possible. There can be few things more disheartening for most people than having to defecate in the open in crowded and uncomfortable conditions.

9.1.1 Needs

It is usually recommended that the ratio of toilets to people should be no more than one per 100 during the early stages of an emergency. This should be improved to one to 20 as quickly as possible for the longer term. The ideal for the users is usually one latrine per family. The issue of access to toilets concerns more than the numbers provided; it also concerns the way in which access is organised. The objective is for every person to be able to reach a toilet they are willing and able to use, which is convenient, hygienic, and comfortable, whatever their age, sex, or physical capacities. See the Sphere Project *Humanitarian Charter and Minimum Standards in Disaster Response*, Chapter 2, section 2.

9.2 Phased response

9.2.1 First phase

Aims

Prevent defecation in the following places:

- by rivers, streams, and lakes and within 50m of water sources
- near water storage and treatment facilities
- uphill of settlements and water sources
- in field crops designed for human consumption
- along public roads
- near public buildings like clinics
- near food storage and preparation centres.

Use mobile sanitation teams to clear up scattered faeces and/or cover with quicklime if necessary (see 9.6.2).

Provide toilets accessible for everyone.

- Aim to provide at least one toilet per 100 people within a few days, and one per 50 people within four weeks.
- To improve access, try to provide a large number of small and well-scattered toilet areas (if public facilities are used), within the limitations demanded by speed and correct siting to avoid contamination of water supplies.
- Aim to have a toilet within 100 metres of each shelter if possible, otherwise many people will be unlikely to use them. This suggests a larger number of smaller toilet blocks or areas, rather than a small number of very large ones.

The above guidelines are intended to help project planning and monitoring, but are only a very rough guide. The important thing is that all the people in the settlement should have access to a toilet nearby when they need it. This may mean that a special effort is needed to find out if there are constraints on access for some people in the community. For instance, children, women, disabled people, poor, or marginalised people may all be denied access for various reasons.

Technical options (see section 9.6)

- Clearing scattered faeces
- Open defecation
- Shallow trench latrines
- Shallow family latrines
- Existing facilities.

Hygiene promotion
During the first phase of an emergency, people almost always have to cope with toilets they are unfamiliar with and which may be unpleasant to use. Hygiene promotion is essential for the best health results from limited and imperfect facilities. As far as possible, try to adapt existing and habitual practices for the people involved, and do things that demand a minimum of behavioural change or new understanding. Try to understand the affected people's situation and their other pre-occupations. Going to the toilet is one of those unavoidable things which people should be able to do as easily and pleasantly as possible, with the minimum of fuss and complication. If this is not possible, it can become a major problem in itself, quite apart from the risk of disease that is involved.

Organisational options
In some situations it may be possible to organise family toilets. However, most usually public toilets in some form have to be organised for first-phase emergencies. The way in which they are organised will affect the progress of future excreta-disposal projects, and it is essential to make it clear to everyone that what is being done is a temporary solution.

9.2.2 Second phase

Aims
After some days, if it is clear that the settlement is likely to remain for at least some weeks, there may be a need for better facilities; if so, they should be provided quickly. If an interim measure is planned, such as blocks of public toilets, there is no point in taking months to build them if they are to be replaced after six months or a year with family latrines. If it is possible to install facilities that can be used in the longer term, this saves spending more time and money later on.

Minimum coverage targets and access
The aim should be to reach Sphere Minimum Standards, i.e. to provide a toilet for every 50 people within four weeks and one for every 20, or one per family, within 3–6 months. They should be within 100 metres of each shelter and, if public facilities are provided, in small blocks rather than large ones, for easy access and a greater sense of ownership for the users.

Organisational options
It is common to provide public toilets at this stage. If it is planned for these to be handed over to the users later on, this should be discussed with the users and the design should be adapted accordingly. It may be possible to start a family-latrine project and avoid building public toilets altogether. In this case, try to get groups of families (up to 10, but preferably no more than four or five) organised around each latrine at the beginning of the project, to spread access as quickly as possible. Group size can be reduced as the project develops. Whatever option

is successful depends very much on what the people involved are ready and willing to make work at that time. Uncertainty about the future, a state of shock, and loss of community may last many weeks, and there might be very little chance of getting a family-latrine programme going. At this stage there may be agencies involved in excreta disposal which do not stay for more than a few months. Co-ordination is very important here, to ensure that what they do brings speedy results, but also that it lays the foundations for more sustainable solutions later on.

Technical options

- Defecation fields
- Shallow trench latrines
- Pit latrines
- Sewage containment/treatment systems
- Existing facilities.

Hygiene promotion
During the first few days and weeks, agency staff should ensure that they are familiar with the following aspects of the affected community:

- normal practices, beliefs, and knowledge about excreta disposal;
- the way the community functions and the structures that exist or develop during the emergency;
- the health situation, particularly patterns of excreta-related disease, and possible epidemics.

This information should be used to design and run hygiene-promotion work, which could be adapted as the situation evolves. See Chapter 7.

9.2.3 Post-emergency phase

Aims
The primary aim for the longer term is to maintain and improve access to toilets which are hygienic, durable, easy to clean, and pleasant to use. A secondary but very important aim may be to reduce dependence on external agencies for providing toilets in the long term, as funding becomes more difficult to secure, and support generally falls away. Reducing dependency on outside agencies implies increased independence for the affected community.

A minimum target is one latrine for not more than 20 people, or one per family, but the way in which access to toilets is organised is as important as the ratio itself.

Organisational options
There are various implications for opting for either family or public toilets in the long term. These are discussed in section 9.3.

Technical options

- Defecation fields (in certain rare circumstances)
- Pit latrines
- Sewage containment and treatment systems
- Existing facilities.

Hygiene promotion
Core staff or volunteers for hygiene education and information gathering should be retained for on-going work. If a family-latrine strategy is chosen, staff will be needed for promoting the project as well as for explaining how to build latrines, where to site them, and how best to use and maintain them.

Monitoring
As during the earlier phases, progress of the excreta-disposal programme over the longer term needs to be monitored, to ensure that resources are directed to where they are most needed and that the project stays on course. Regular monitoring is needed even after targets have been reached, to ensure that access to good-quality toilets is maintained, and to anticipate problems such as latrines becoming full. Satisfactory situations can quickly deteriorate if support is not sustained. See section 9.6.

9.3 Organisational options

9.3.1 Introduction

The two main options are usually public or family facilities. For the purposes of this guide they are defined as follows. **Public toilets** are designed and built, maintained and cleaned by an agency (government or non-government), on behalf of the users. The toilets belong to the agency and not to the users. **Family toilets** are usually built by the users, with or without materials provided by an agency, and with or without a design provided by an agency, usually without payment for the work involved. Family toilets may, in practice, be used by several families, but the important thing is that the users are a defined and organised group who have a degree of ownership of the toilet. A compromise between the two may be called a **communal latrine**. This is a public toilet which is managed by the community as a shared resource: perhaps a latrine managed by a market committee, or school toilets managed by the school authorities and parents.

Table 9.1 on page 144 presents some of the advantages and disadvantages of each approach. Whatever organisational option is chosen, the facilities must be well designed and well built, or they will fail to serve their primary purpose.

9.3.2 Public toilets

Applications
Public toilets can be used in an emergency to provide an adequate short-term level of access relatively quickly. They do not provide an ideal long-term solution, for reasons outlined in the table on the next page , though in some circumstances there may be no other option.

They differ very little technically from family toilets, but need a very different type of organisation. Essentially, they are toilets built and managed by an agency, as opposed to being built and managed by the users. They can be built relatively quickly if a large workforce, suitable tools, and appropriate materials are available. In rocky areas it may be far easier to build public latrines using heavy machinery than for refugees to dig their own pits with hand tools. Where soil conditions demand unusually sophisticated latrine design and construction, better technical results may be achieved by using a centralised workforce to build and manage the latrines.

On the other hand, long-term costs of public latrines may remain high, and there are social implications to be considered — see table 9.1. If public toilets are chosen as an intermediate option, the programme should be planned and explained clearly to the population, to avoid making a family-toilet project more difficult later on.

Design considerations
All technical options may be suitable, depending on the urgency of the situation, access to materials and equipment, cultural preference, etc. But whatever the technical option chosen, public toilets should satisfy the following criteria. They should be:

- designed and located in ways that are culturally appropriate, e.g. for sitters or squatters, washers or wipers, and located for privacy;
- accessible for easy emptying if that is needed: within 20m of access roads, or alongside access paths if mechanical emptying is planned;
- easy to clean;
- robust and hard-wearing;
- built in such a way that materials (particularly plastic sheeting) are hard to steal;
- easy for children, old, and disabled people to use, i.e. some should have handrails for support, some latrines should have smaller drop holes, latrines should not be too dark inside;
- safe to use, particularly at night (lighting should be considered);
- provided with water close by for washing hands;
- with separate sections or separate blocks for men and for women;
- in blocks as small and scattered as cost, speed, and technical considerations allow (within 50m of shelters, no more than eight toilets per block if possible).

Implementation and management

Large numbers of construction workers are usually needed to build public toilets, particularly if they have to be built quickly and if there is a lot of digging involved. Work on a large number of sites has to be supervised, and problems often occur with the control of purchase, storage, and use of materials.

Public toilets need regular cleaning and maintenance by specially allocated staff, who need cleaning materials and protective clothing. Their work needs supervision to ensure that people are not discouraged from using dirty and smelly toilets and that they are not a disease risk in themselves. Users may need training and encouragement to use the toilets hygienically.

Table 9.1 Advantages and disadvantages of public and family toilets

Public toilets		Family toilets	
Advantages	*Disadvantages*	*Advantages*	*Disadvantages*
Speed of construction			
Can be constructed very fast in an emergency with a well-trained and well-equipped team.	Speed of construction is limited by the number of staff involved and their equipment.	Large numbers can be built very quickly, as many families are involved.	It may take considerable time to start a family-toilet programme, including time taken to train families.
Technical quality			
Design and construction are centrally managed, so quality of construction is easier to control.	Innovative ideas from the users themselves may be missed.	The ingenuity of users is applied to technical problems.	It is more difficult to ensure good siting and construction.
Construction costs			
Large-scale construction techniques can be used. It is easier to control the use of materials and to achieve economies of scale.	Construction labour must be paid for.	Construction labour and maybe some local materials (e.g. grass for superstructures) are free of charge	Families may not have the time or the skills or the family members available to do the work themselves, or this might be a financial drain for them.
Maintenance costs			
Maintenance, repair, and replacement costs are easier to predict and plan.	It may be more expensive to maintain the staff levels needed for cleaning and maintenance.	Users take responsibility for cleaning, maintenance, some repairs, and even emptying.	Recurrent costs are more unpredictable, e.g. costs of replacing or emptying large numbers of full latrines.

Table 9.1 Advantages and disadvantages of public and family toilets (continued)

Public toilets		Family toilets	
Advantages	Disadvantages	Advantages	Disadvantages
Technical possibilities			
Heavy equipment and specialised techniques can be used on difficult sites (e.g. rocky ground).			Families may not be able to dig in hard rock, or build raised latrines or lay sewers in areas of high ground-water.
Cleaning and hygiene			
Users do not have to clean toilets.	Toilets are often dirty, unless cleaning is very well organised. Toilets may be less accessible, so less likely to be used. They may be more insecure, particularly for women. Users have little influence on the design.	Toilets are often cleaner, and if they are not clean then it may be easier for users to get the cleaning improved. Toilets are often more accessible (closer to shelters) and safer.	Toilets may be more difficult to clean. Many users may prefer not to be responsible for construction, cleaning, and maintenance.
Cleaning of toilets is usually more easily monitored by the agency.	A greater mix of people uses each toilet, increasing the risk of disease spread.	Use is restricted to a more confined group of people, so reducing the risk of disease spread.	Cleaning and hygiene may be more difficult for the agency to monitor.
Development issues			
Public toilets provide an opportunity for contact with users through demonstration of construction and use techniques.	People may lose or not get the habit of looking after their own toilet. This has implications for the post-emergency situation.	People keep or develop the habit of looking after their own toilet. Ideas and techniques useful for return or resettlement can be introduced.	

Handing over public toilets to groups of users

If it is planned to hand over public toilets to groups of user families, try to make this clear to the population as early as possible. In Kahindo camp in Goma, Zaire, people remained unclear about responsibility for managing public latrines that had been handed over to them, because this was done too quickly and without enough discussion. Several months after the latrines were handed over, many were falling down and abandoned altogether. Each individual toilet in a block should be handed over, in a good state of repair, to one family or a small group of families, and their responsibilities and rights regarding the toilet should be explained and agreed upon. In the case of a block of pit latrines, think about who is to be responsible for emptying the pit if it becomes full, or who is to do general repairs. If these things are not thought through and made clear to all parties at the time of the handover, problems will be created for the future.

9.3.3 Family toilets

Applications
For Oxfam, family toilets (usually family latrines) are the preferred option for long-term situations, and may also be appropriate in the early stages of an emergency. The primary reasons for preferring family latrines are, first, that each one has a more confined group of users, thus reducing the chances of cross-contamination; and, second, that enabling people to build their own latrines gives them much greater control over this very important and personal domain. Even during first-phase emergencies, it may be possible to provide families with small wooden or plastic slabs to build their own temporary latrines. This was done in Kibumba camp in Goma in 1994 and in Cukurça camp in Turkey in 1991. There are mixed opinions on the success of this approach, however, and family latrines are usually confined to later stages of emergencies, although some families will always prefer to make their own arrangements right from the start.

Design considerations
Virtually any of the available technical options could be used to provide family toilets, except defecation areas, where it is not possible to designate individual family or group toilets. Whatever the technical option chosen, if family toilets are to be built by the users, they should be

- easy for the users to understand, build, use, and look after with the minimum of external support, and technology that is easy for staff to understand and explain;
- appropriate in terms of culture and practice, as for public toilets, though the users have more control over the design if they build the toilets themselves;
- designed in a way that does not involve users in a lot of recurrent work and expense, and built of materials which are very durable if the toilets are to last a long time;
- hygienic, safe, and attractive to use for all people in the family.

Hygiene promotion
The implementation of a family-latrine project should start with informing the population about what is planned, being clear about roles and responsibilities, what the agency will provide, and what is expected of the users. At this stage it may be necessary to do some intensive hygiene-promotion work to educate

people about the value of toilets for their health, and to encourage their participation in the project. This is usually best done through the staff who will be implementing the project, as well as leaders, other agencies, and outreach structures such as community health facilities.

The degree to which the community participates in the work will depend on people's background and the situation in the camp. It is not always appropriate to build a project on the assumption of a high level of community participation. Projects that successfully involve the community depend on good preparation and communication. In some situations, families may build their own toilets whether or not the agency assists them, and this can be encouraged, provided that the toilets are built and sited so as to avoid creating health risks.

Monitoring

Family latrines may fill up during the life of the settlement, particularly if many people are using each one, and soil conditions make it difficult to dig adequately deep pits. Such latrines have to be replaced or emptied at some stage. If there is space, a new pit can be dug nearby and the slab and superstructure transferred, while the old pit is back-filled with soil. If the second latrine needs replacing after some time, the first pit can be emptied, with the necessary precautions taken to avoid contamination, and then re-used. Slabs and superstructures may need replacing at some time. Try to be clear at the beginning of the programme about who is to be responsible for rebuilding and repairing family latrines. See section 9.6.

Shared family latrines

In most emergency situations and even many stable situations, families share toilets; this may be extended to quite large groups of people using communal toilets. Where and when people from several families are able to get together to manage a shared facility, this can be a very good way to provide access to a toilet without delay, and without many of the disadvantages of public toilets. Shared family latrines based on single cubicle pits have been successful in Rwandan camps in Tanzania and Zaire. Four or five families would share responsibility for construction, maintenance, and cleaning. When latrines are used by more families than this, they become very difficult for people to manage together. This organisation is much easier where plots for shelters and latrines are laid out in a way that helps to identify latrines with families within a shared space.

9.4 Staffing needs

A large number of people are usually needed to start the emergency sanitation project, often doing more organisation and communication work than construction. This may change if the agency starts latrine construction, when people with different skills may be needed. If a family-latrine project is to be run, then different skills again will be required, with more staff engaged in promoting community involvement and helping people to site and build latrines, others managing the purchase and distribution of materials, and others making concrete slabs, etc. Job descriptions should be flexible enough to take this into account, and some changes in personnel will usually be needed.

A typical staffing structure for an excreta-disposal project in an emergency settlement of 50,000 people is shown in Table 9.2.

Table 9.2 Example of staff needs for an excreta-disposal project for 50,000 people

Phase	Main activities[1]	Staff type	Nos.
I: days	*Setting up and running defecation fields, hygiene promotion*		
	Site management, administration, logistics, etc.	Manager, storekeeper, buyer, administrator, driver	5
	Setting up 10 defecation fields	Labourers and team leaders[2]	110
	Maintaining 10 defecation fields	Labourers and team leaders[2]	60
	Hygiene promotion and information exchange	Hygiene promoters and team leaders[3]	55
II: weeks	*Constructing and running public pit latrines*		
	Site management, administration, logistics, etc.	Manager, storekeepers, buyer, administrator, drivers	8
	Construction of public pit latrines	Skilled workers, labourers, and team leaders	210
	Cleaning and maintaining public pit latrines	Cleaners and team leaders	85
	Hygiene promotion and information exchange	Hygiene promoters and team leaders[3]	55
III: months	*Family pit-latrine programme*		
	Site management, administration, logistics, etc.	Manager, storekeepers, buyer, administrator, drivers	8
	Advising population on latrine siting and construction	Latrine technicians and team leaders[4]	55
	Concrete latrine-slab production	Masons, labourers, and team leaders	22
	Hygiene promotion and information exchange. Programme monitoring	Hygiene promoters and team leaders[3]	55

1 These activities overlap as the situation and programme develop. For example, defecation fields will be managed while the public latrines are being built. The family latrines may be started before the public latrine programme is finished.

2 Workers setting up and then maintaining defecation fields may be the same staff, who move straight on to maintenance as soon as the defecation fields go into use.

3 See Chapter 7 for notes on hygiene-promotion staff.

4 Latrine technicians may have a role which overlaps somewhat with that of the hygiene promoters, and it may be possible to combine the two jobs.

9.5 Monitoring latrine programmes

It is very important, for monitoring the use of materials and the progress of the project, that adequate and correct records are kept. Commonly figures on latrine provision look good, but do not reflect the true picture, as many of the latrines recorded are not actually in use, because construction is not completed, they are damaged, they are full, or they have collapsed. An accounting system is needed to keep track of new latrines being built (at different stages of construction), latrines in use, pits that are full, superstructures that have fallen down or blown away, etc. This should relate to the size of the population covered in each section of the settlement and to the quantities of materials used. Use of toilets may also need to be monitored, if this is a potential problem (for example, where a new type of toilet is introduced to the community). See Chapter 7 on hygiene promotion.

9.6 Technical options

The aim of this section is not to give a detailed technical description of available technical options, but to present a brief survey of options with some guidance to help you to choose the most suitable one for a particular situation, and to offer some notes on the practical implications of that choice. Several detailed technical manuals are available, and some of these are listed at the end of this chapter. Of particular relevance are *Engineering in Emergencies*, published by RedR; *Public Health Technician in Emergency Situation*, published by Médecins sans Frontières; and Oxfam's internal Guidelines on Emergency Excreta Disposal.

9.6.1 Adapting existing facilities

In many situations where urban areas are affected by disasters, the existing facilities such as sewers, septic tanks, and pit latrines may still be usable. However, they may be damaged, or inadequate for the number of people they have to serve if the area receives a large number of displaced people. A rapid assessment is needed to decide whether it is worth trying to use the existing facilities or whether to replace them with something more simple. Points to consider include the following.

Sewerage systems

Water supply for sewerage systems: Most sewerage systems need at least 20–40 litres of water per user per day to be flushed into the system to keep the sewage running. Where this volume of piped water is not available, users may be encouraged to use untreated water from another supply for flushing toilets, or it may be possible to keep sewers clear by flushing them out regularly with water from streams or rivers.

Power supply for pumped sewerage systems: In cities in flat areas, some parts of the sewerage system may have pumping stations, which may need a back-up power supply to keep the system running if there are general power failures. This is likely to be a major undertaking.

Power supply for sewage-treatment works: The treatment works may need a back-up power supply to avoid discharging untreated sewage into water courses and possibly creating environmental and environmental health problems.

Structural damage: Even when there has been extensive structural damage, it may be possible to isolate certain parts of a sewer system and keep others in service, or use mobile pumps or tankers to by-pass blockages or breakages.

Adding toilets to existing sewers: It may be possible to build blocks of temporary toilets which are flushed into an existing sewer, or which may be built directly over the sewer in the case of dry latrines. In the latter case, the sewer will need frequent flushing to keep it clear. Temporary toilets with holding tanks may be emptied by tankers, which then discharge into a sewer.

Septic tanks and pit latrines

Structural damage: Earthquakes and floods may cause septic tanks and pit latrines to collapse, crack, or subside, in which case it may be quicker and cheaper to replace them with new structures.

Adding toilets: The most time-consuming part of building latrines and septic tanks is constructing the pit, lining, and cover. It may be possible to build additional toilets over or adjacent to existing septic tanks or latrine pits, to increase access rapidly.

Emptying: When the population of an existing settlement is greatly increased after a disaster, existing latrines and septic tanks will need to be emptied more frequently, so provision should be made for this.

9.6.2 Mobile sanitation teams

Where there is a lot of scattered faeces in a settlement or along a road, or where it is not possible, for any reason, to establish an effective defecation system, it may be necessary to employ teams of people to disinfect and/or remove faeces. These teams should be provided with protective clothing and washing facilities, and tools such as shovels, rakes, and wheelbarrows. If faeces are to be disinfected, they should be scattered with quicklime, which also dries the surface of the faeces and discourages flies. Faeces may be buried in pits and covered with at least 500mm of compacted soil.

9.6.3 Open defecation systems

Application
Defecation fields are a short-term solution for excreta disposal while longer-term measures are being prepared. Their purpose is to contain excreta within defined borders, rather than allow them to be deposited all around the emergency settlement. They consist of defined areas in which defecation and urination are allowed to take place. The areas are selected so that they are convenient for the users but create little or no pollution of potential and existing sources of water and food.

While simple in concept and construction, their operation requires careful control, to keep cross-infection to a minimum. Also, since defecation fields are in use during the early stages of development of the settlement, the disaster-affected community requires firm control to ensure that defecation takes place in the designated areas. This is particularly so for people who are not used to defecating in public.

Options
The two usual options are open defecation fields and trench defecation fields. The principles of operation are basically the same: people are encouraged to defecate within a clearly marked area of land, using one strip of that land at a time, and moving regularly on to fresh strips to avoid an excessive accumulation of excreta in any one place. With **open defecation fields**, at least some of the faeces are left in the open on the soil surface. This system is better suited to dry climates, where sunshine and heat quickly dry up and sterilise any excreta left on the surface, though people should always be encouraged to bury their faeces where possible.

In most situations, **trench defecation fields** are far more appropriate in terms of hygiene and convenience for users. Here, shallow trenches are provided so that the faeces can more easily be covered over by the users, and this system should be used if there is time, labour, and equipment available to do so.

Where land is very scarce, **intensive defecation areas** may be needed, where the surface is regularly cleared of excreta, and cleaned so that it can be reused.

Location and soil conditions
- Locate defecation fields at least 30 metres from habitable buildings, but as centrally as possible (within 100 metres of shelters if possible).
- Site them on land sloping away from the settlement and surface-water sources. Consideration should be given to the direction of prevailing winds, to reduce nuisance caused by odour. Areas subject to flooding or containing running water should be avoided.
- The soil should be easy to dig, so that faeces can be buried.
- The site should be provided with adequate surface drains to divert surface water running across it from above and to collect and contain it.

- The location of the fields must be discussed with the refugees before finalising plans, to ensure that the fields comply, as far as possible, with their customs.
- The site should be lit at night and guarded to reduce the risk of attacks on women.

Size

The larger the area available, the less dense will be the excreta on the ground and hence the less chance of cross-contamination. Provided that the site is well managed, allow approximately 0.25m² (i.e. 500 × 500mm) per day per person. (This excludes access paths.) This means 250m² per 10,000 people per day, or nearly 2 hectares per week. For defecation trenches, allow 3.5m of trench per 100 users. Trenches will need to be replaced as they fill up.

Setting up defecation fields

Open defecation fields: A strip of land about 1500mm wide is demarcated on either side of the access path. Users are allowed to defecate within that strip until it is fully utilised. People should be encouraged to defecate on one side only of the strip, so that space is available for walking without treading on fresh excreta. People should be encouraged to bury their excreta if possible. However, they will need small spades for this.

When the strip is full, another strip is opened up for use. If possible, the next strip should not be adjacent to the last one, to reduce the nuisance from smell and flies. The excreta in the full strip may be left to decompose, but it is much better if they can be covered with soil daily, to prevent flies breeding and to reduce odour.

When a field is being used by a large number of people, it may be better to have a number of strips open at the same time. This will allow individuals to separate themselves from one another, to provide some level of privacy.

Strips should not extend too far from the access path (about 20 metres), since the farthest ends will not be fully utilised. Better results may be obtained by encouraging people to enter along one path and leave by another.

Trench defecation fields: A small trench 150mm deep and 200 to 300mm wide is dug along the middle of the strip. The spoil is thrown on the down-hill side of the trench, since it is easier to squat facing up-hill. One worker would be able to dig up to 50 metres of such trench per day. Allow sufficient digging tools for this. The users walk along the strip on the opposite side to the spoil and excrete directly into the trench. When the bottom of a section of trench is fully covered with excreta, it is filled in. Only short lengths of trench should be opened for use at any one time, to encourage the full utilisation of the trench in a short time. As with open defecation, it may be appropriate to have a number of trenches open at the same time.

With both open and trench defecation, the field can be used only once; therefore it is important that efforts should be made immediately either to find other defecation fields or to identify an alternative longer-term solution.

Hygiene promotion

Defecation fields will work well only with the full co-operation of the community — and even then people will require continued encouragement and help. Each field should have at least two persons present at all times to guide individual users to the right area and ensure that other areas of the field are not used. More staff are required to move around the camp, informing people where they should go to defecate and explaining how the system works and why it is necessary. It is important that all new arrivals are contacted as soon as they are settled, with further visits to ensure that the message is fully understood and put into practice. Advisory staff can also check for signs of defecation in other areas and attempt to prevent its occurrence.

In order to encourage good hygiene practices, a water point, with soap, should be placed near the exit from the defecation fields, so that users can wash their hands. If no soap is available, or if there is a risk of epidemic, then the water should be chlorinated at a rate of 0.05 per cent of chlorine. Good drainage away from this point is essential, in order to encourage its use. It may be necessary to provide anal-cleansing materials, as for other forms of public toilets.

Covering the excreta

Where defecation is on to the ground, faeces may be covered by digging up the adjoining soil and throwing it on top of the excreta or by carting in soil or sand from another area. The former method is the easiest, but it cannot be used where there is little or no top-soil, or where defecation has been indiscriminate. All excreta should be covered with at least 100mm of soil as soon as possible, to prevent the breeding of flies and reduce odours.

The excreta should not be moved from the field, unless space is very limited and more intensive defecation areas are used.

9.6.4 Pit latrines: general considerations

Pit latrines, in one form or another, are the most common and appropriate type of toilet for most emergency situations. There are a number of factors to consider when planning a pit-latrine programme. They apply to all of the types of latrine that follow. For more detailed information on latrines, see the suggested reading list at the end of this chapter.

Volume of excreta

In emergencies, latrines are generally intensively used and can quickly fill before the excreta have had time to reduce in volume through decomposition and other processes. Assume a total volume of 1–2 litres per person per day, including urine but excluding anal-cleansing materials. In permeable soils, assume a solids-addition rate of 0.5 litres per person per day. Over a longer period, allowing for a reduction in solids volume, assume a sludge-accumulation rate of between 50 and 150 litres per person per year, depending on the anal-cleansing material used, the climate, and the wetness of the sludge in the pit.

Ground conditions

It is essential to investigate soil conditions carefully before selecting a latrine option. Soil that is unsuitable for latrines is a significant drawback for any potential emergency settlement. Dig trial pits by hand or with an auger in different places around the site, to take account of variations in soil type. Carry out percolation tests and simple soil-identification tests to identify problem soils. The main ground-condition problems are the following.

Rocky areas: Hard rock at or near the surface may limit the possible depth of pits and therefore their life. It may be necessary to raise sealed walls above the ground surface, to increase the effective volume of the pit. Alternating twin pit latrines are also an option. These options are difficult to implement rapidly, as they need skilled construction techniques and substantial amounts of building materials. Another option is to use power tools to dig pits, or drilling rigs to drill borehole latrine pits.

Areas with shallow ground-water: Similar problems and possible solutions exist as for rocky areas. In addition to raised pits and alternating twin pits, it may be possible to build sealed pits, effectively holding tanks, which need to be emptied frequently.

Low-permeability soils: If the soil is not sufficiently permeable to absorb the normal liquid volumes added through excretion and, in some cases, anal washing, then the latrine pits will fill with liquid. Users should be encouraged not to add liquid unnecessarily, and special care may be needed to reduce mosquito breeding. Large-diameter pits tend to absorb liquids more effectively, and pit volume may be increased as above. In some cases it may be possible to dig a second pit close to the first one, to receive excess liquid via an overflow pipe.

Unstable soils: It may be necessary to line latrine pits partially or fully, to keep the walls from collapsing. Ensure that the top 500mm, usually the most unstable layer, are given an impermeable lining to help to prevent surface-water infiltration. Use lining materials suitable for the life of the latrine. Possible materials include bamboo, geo-textiles, grass mats, timber, stone, mortar, concrete, and brick. Circular pits are more stable than square pits or trenches. In areas of high ground-water, it may be necessary to line the pit with an impermeable floor and walls to reduce ground-water pollution. Ensure that the lining is sufficiently heavy to resist floating, if the water table rises above the pit bottom when the pit is empty.

Ground-water pollution

Pits dug in the unsaturated zone above the ground-water table: In most soils, allow at least 1500mm between the bottom of the pit and the ground-water table, to reduce the number of pathogens reaching the ground-water. Increase this distance in high-rainfall areas and in coarse or fissured soils.

Pits dug in the saturated zone below the water table: The horizontal movement of pollutants, once in the saturated zone, is far greater than their vertical movement. Therefore allow at least 30m from the latrine to any ground-water source in this case, and increase this distance for coarse or fissured soils. Ensure that wells and boreholes nearby are adequately sealed from the ground level to the level of pollution.

Fly and mosquito control
Blowflies may breed in latrine pits, and measures should be taken in dense settlements to reduce this. These include the use of VIP (ventilated improved pit) latrines (see 9.6.10 below), pour-flush latrines, latrines with tight-fitting covers, or frequent covering of faeces with soil or ashes. In latrine pits that are saturated because of a high ground-water table or impermeable soils, breeding Culicene mosquitoes may be a problem. Possible solutions include using VIP or pour-flush latrines, or the use of polystyrene beads for killing larvae in the pit.

Slabs
The most time-consuming and expensive part of much latrine construction is the slab, which serves to cover and protect the pit and take the weight of the user and, in some cases, part or all of the superstructure. Slabs may be made of planks, local timbers, stones and earth, concrete, ferro-cement, plastic or brick arches.

Traditional timber and earth slabs: These have the advantage of being familiar to many rural people, rapid to put in place, easy to use on pits which may be of irregular shape and size, and cheap in financial terms. However, they need finishing with mortar or an additional cement or plastic slab to make them hygienic and easy to clean; they may cost a lot in environmental terms; and they usually need replacing after a number of months.

Wooden planks: These are often used to build public latrines in an emergency. They can be used to span large and irregular-shaped pits, with suitable timber supports, they can be made rapidly and simply with local skills, and can be fairly durable if they are treated with a suitable preservative. Their disadvantages include the possible environmental costs of locally bought timbers, which may come from sensitive forest areas; the uncertainty that users may feel about walking on a wooden platform over a pit; and the difficulties they pose for sealing pits and for keeping clean. These last two problems can be overcome by covering the slabs with plastic sheeting, although this may encourage the timbers to rot. A plastic or concrete slab may be placed on top of the timber slab, to provide a hygienic squatting plate.

Plastic slabs: A number of international and local companies manufacture plastic latrine slabs, either for spanning the whole latrine pit, or for use with timber or other supports. They have been successfully used on trench latrines to provide a large number of toilets very fast. The advantages of plastic slabs are that they are extremely rapid to use; they provide a hygienic and easily cleaned squatting plate; they do not need a slab-production programme to be mounted in an emergency situation; they are easily removed and transported when people move; and they are long-lasting and hard-wearing. Their disadvantages include their relatively high cost; the need, generally, to use timber or other materials to support the slabs, which tend to be too small to span a pit; and the springy feel they often give when walking on them.

Concrete slabs: Concrete slabs are generally the preferred option for the longer term. They are relatively cheap, using materials and labour which are generally locally available; they are hard-wearing, easy to clean (if well finished), and feel solid and safe to the users; and rural people, once introduced to them, may use them in the future. However, it takes time to produce concrete slabs, so they are unsuitable for the early phases of an emergency, unless contingency stocks are prepared, or they are available on the local market; they are costly and difficult to transport; their production requires careful planning and management; and they require careful control of pit size and shape.

Several options for emergency latrine-slab design are available, including various designs of full-sized slabs, and small slabs (for example, the Sanplat), which can be used on top of a traditional slab or a timber slab. When setting up and running a slab-production workshop, consider the following points.

- Gear workshop capacity to the speed at which minimum standards of latrine can be reached.
- Where will you obtain materials, especially sand and gravel, of the right quality? Will the users be involved in supplying any of the materials?
- What staff are available, and what are their skills?
- How will the workshop be designed and constructed?
- How will slabs be transported to the latrines? It may be possible to cast the slab beside each pit, as is often done in rural areas, rather than casting them in a central workshop.

Superstructures

To the users, the superstructure is probably the most important part of the latrine, as this provides the privacy essential for comfort and dignity. The materials and techniques used for the superstructure should generally not be very different from those used for people's shelters. If people are able to build their own shelters, they are generally also able to build their own latrine superstructures.

Some latrine designs demand a roof on the superstructure. For instance, VIP latrines usually require a roof. A roof is necessary where slabs need protection from the rain, where rainfall should be kept from entering the pit, or in cold and very wet climates. In other cases it may be better not to have a roof.

Doors may be used, and many people prefer doors they can lock to keep the latrine private. Otherwise, spiral-shaped walls allow privacy without the need for a closing door.

Emptying latrines

In areas where latrines fill rapidly because of soil conditions or high usage rates, it may be necessary to empty them periodically. Where appropriate, the latrine should be designed and located to make this easy. Mechanical emptying is the most hygienic method. The most suitable form of pump, where latrines receive significant amounts of large and hard solids such as stones and rags, is a vacuum pump. Small models of vacuum pump, suitable for reaching latrines in densely populated emergency settlements, are available, though their use in emergency situations has been very limited so far. Impeller and progressive cavity pumps tend not to deal well with large solids. Emptying may be done by hand, provided that adequate supervision, protective clothing, and washing facilities are provided for the operators. The sludge may be transported off the site and disposed of into an existing treatment works, sludge ponds, or a landfill site with solid waste. Alternatively, where there is space on site, the sludge may be dumped into a pit dug near the latrine and then covered over. This is a less advisable option.

9.6.5 Bucket latrines

The bucket latrine system involves users excreting into buckets with tight-fitting lids, which should be emptied at least daily, and the contents disposed of in a sewerage system or an improvised treatment/disposal system, such as a landfill site or waste-stabilisation ponds. If possible, a disinfectant should be used in the bucket to reduce the risk of contamination; a deodorant/disinfectant liquid, as used in camping toilets, helps to make the toilet more pleasant to use. It is better, to avoid spillage of excreta when emptying the bucket into a transport container at each household, to simply replace the full bucket with a washed and disinfected empty one.

This type of system has rarely been used in emergencies and may be difficult to use safely in practice, but could be a useful option for situations where it is possible to organise a reliable system of collection and disposal, and where users find the method acceptable and easy to use.

9.6.6 Shallow family latrines

During the first days and weeks following a disaster, many people try to build some sort of latrine for themselves, using materials to hand. It is sometimes possible to help them to build more hygienic latrines which are less likely to contaminate the settlement by providing plastic, wooden, or concrete slabs and advice on locating and constructing their latrines. As they are shallow, these latrines can be dug very quickly, and can provide toilets which are convenient for family use and should last a family of five for several weeks. The disadvantages are that it is very difficult to provide a very large number of slabs in a short space of time; it is difficult to control the use of the slabs, the location of the pits, and the closing and back-filling of the pits when full. Problems may be caused by having a large number of closed temporary pits within the settlement, if they are unmarked or they take up space which is needed later for more permanent latrines.

Technique

- Pits are dug about 500 × 500 × 500mm.
- Slabs should be large enough to cover the pit and allow at least 150mm to rest on the soil on two opposite edges.
- Pits should be closed and back-filled with compacted soil when they are full to within 200mm of the ground surface.

Notes

- Families may need guidance to ensure that pits are correctly located and slabs are correctly installed.
- Families may build superstructures themselves.
- If it is decided that families should not build temporary latrines, then this needs to be explained carefully so as not to discourage future involvement in a more permanent family-latrine programme.
- Fly breeding is unlikely to be a problem in temporary latrines, provided that slabs have covers for the squatting holes, that they are used, that they are not used for longer than a month, and are back-filled with at least 10cm of soil.

9.6.7 Shallow trench latrines

Shallow trench latrines allow a large number of toilets to be provided rapidly, for temporary communal or public use, in an emergency. They may be dug by hand, or by mechanical excavation. They are far more sanitary than defecation fields.

Technique

- Site as for defecation fields, to avoid nuisance and reduce the risk of contaminating water sources and living areas.
- Shallow trenches should be 300mm wide and 900–1500mm deep. Allow 3.5m for every 100 users.
- Place planks along each edge of the trench, to prevent the edges collapsing and give users a firm foothold.
- Fence off the area (for example with plastic sheeting) for privacy and to keep animals out. Provide separate areas for men and for women.
- Provide hand-washing facilities.
- When the excreta reach about 300mm from the ground surface, back-fill the trench with compacted soil, mark the spot, and dig another trench.
- Users cover their faeces with a little soil, and staff periodically clean the foot-boards and cover the pit contents with 50–100mm of soil.

Notes

- Staff are needed to ensure that people know how to use the latrine correctly, and to clean the foot-boards and add soil from time to time.
- The more privacy that can be provided, the more likely the latrine is to be used.
- Lay wooden or plastic slabs across the trench, if available, to make use safer and more pleasant, particularly in wet weather.

9.6.8 Deep trench latrines

Deep trench latrines take longer than shallow trench latrines to construct, but they provide more sanitary and durable toilets. They are particularly suitable for mechanical excavation, but may be dug rapidly by hand with a large workforce.

Technique

- Site as for defecation fields, to avoid nuisance and reduce the risk of contaminating water sources and living areas.
- Deep trenches should be 800mm wide and up to 2000mm deep. A typical deep trench latrine is 6m long.
- In unstable soils, line the trench sides with timber or other supports. Lay a 1000mm side-strip of plastic sheeting along the trench edges, with 500mm hanging down into the trench and 500mm on the ground along the trench edge to protect it from erosion.
- The trench is covered with timbers or a series of plastic or concrete slabs, which may need additional timber supports.
- Provide a superstructure over the pit, with one cubicle per metre of trench.
- Add a roof if rain is expected.
- Provide hand-washing facilities.
- Backfill the trench with compacted soil when it is full to within 500mm of the ground surface.

Notes

As for shallow trench latrines.

9.6.9 Simple pit latrines

Simple pit latrines are semi-permanent toilets made from placing a squatting slab with a tight-fitting lid over a deep hole in the ground. The superstructure may be made of local materials or plastic sheeting and timber. Simple pit latrines are the toilets used by many people in rural areas in poor countries. This type of latrine is suitable for family-latrine programmes in emergency settlements, because it is simple to build and maintain by the users. It is not easy to control flies in this type of latrine, unless the squatting-hole lids are used rigorously. There is often a bad smell inside the latrine superstructure, particularly when the pit contents are very wet. It is possible to upgrade simple pit latrines to VIP latrines, if, when the slab is made, a plugged hole is left for insertion of a vent pipe.

Technique

- Site to avoid ground-water pollution, and at least 6m from shelters.
- The pit volume should be chosen according to the planned life of the latrine, assuming a solids-accumulation rate of 0.04m^3 per user per year, and allowing 500mm of free space above the maximum level of excreta before emptying or back-filling the pit.
- The slab may be made of timbers and earth, planks or concrete, and should be large enough to take the required weights and to seal the pit.
- The slab should have a tight-fitting lid to reduce fly breeding.
- Line the pit if necessary.
- Ensure that the pit is protected from erosion by providing cut-off drainage and raising excavated soil up around the pit edges.

9.6.10 Ventilated improved pit (VIP) latrines

Properly constructed and maintained VIP latrines have two main advantages over simple pit latrines: they reduce odours inside the latrine, so encouraging use, and they control flies and mosquitoes. They are more expensive and more complicated to construct than simple pit latrines and, unless they are maintained, they are not effective for fly control. They are rarely suitable for the emergency phase.

Technique

- As for simple pit latrines. In addition:
- Add a vent pipe with an internal diameter of 100–150mm, capped with mosquito screen, extending 500mm above the superstructure roof, to control odours, flies, and mosquitoes. The vent pipe may be made of PVC, brick, or other suitable material.
- The superstructure should be sufficiently dark on the inside to ensure that the strongest source of light entering the latrine pit is via the vent pipe, for fly control, but sufficiently light to make it easy to see inside.

Notes

- Entering a dimly lit toilet may discourage children in particular. It is not necessary to exclude light from the superstructure, if a loose-fitting lid is placed over the squatting hole to shade the pit.
- It is important that the mosquito screen on the top of the vent pipe is replaced if it is lost or damaged.

9.6.11 Pour-flush latrines

In cultures where anal washing is the norm, pour-flush latrines are a suitable variant of the simple pit latrine. They provide good control of flies and mosquitoes because of the water trap in the squatting plate, and they can be flushed with a very small quantity of water (1–2 litres).

Technique

- As for simple pit latrines. In addition:
- Pour-flush latrine slabs are usually made of concrete, with a pre-formed plastic or cement pan set in.
- Pour-flush latrines may be built with the pit off-set from the superstructure, to avoid the need for a load-bearing slab over the pit.
- In low-permeability soils, pour-flush latrines may need frequent emptying or additional soak-away pits to deal with the excess liquid.

9.6.12 Twin-pit latrines

In areas of high ground-water where contamination of drinking water is to be avoided, or where space for replacing semi-permanent pit latrines is limited, twin-pit latrines are an option for long-term excreta disposal. They consist of two relatively shallow pits, side by side, separated by a solid wall, each pit large enough to contain two years' worth of accumulated solids. One pit is used at a time; when full, it is closed off and the other one is used. At the end of the second two years, the first pit may be emptied and the contents used safely for gardening, if required. These latrines need relatively large amounts of materials and are substantially more complicated to build than most other types.

9.7 Options for problem sites

Table 9.3 suggests a number of options for short-term and long-term excreta-disposal solutions on problem sites.

Table 9.3: Short-term and long-term options for excreta disposal on difficult sites

	Problem		
	Lack of space	High water table	Rocky ground
Short term	Bucket latrines Intensive defecation areas	Defecation fields Bucket latrines Shallow trench latrines	Defecation fields Bucket latrines and emptying Raised latrines and de-sludging
Longer term	Twin-pit latrines Lined single-pit latrines and de-sludging Sewered system	Fully lined and watertight latrines or septic tanks and de-sludging Raised latrines and de-sludging Sewered system	Raised latrines and de-sludging Sewered system

Further reading

J. Davis and R. Lambert (1995) *Engineering in Emergencies: A practical guide for relief workers*, Chapter 8, London: RedR/IT Publications

MSF (1992) *Public Health Technician in Emergency Situation*, first edition, Chapter 2, Paris: Médicins sans Frontières

Oxfam (1998), Guidelines on Emergency Excreta Disposal (draft, unpublished, not for general circulation), Oxford: Oxfam GB

J. Pickford (1995) *Low-cost Sanitation: A survey of practical experience*, London: IT Publications

Sphere Project (1999, forthcoming) *Humanitarian Charter and Minimum Standards in Disaster Response*, Chapter 2, Section 2: 'Excreta disposal', published in Geneva by the Steering Committee for Humanitarian Response (SCHR) and Interaction; e-mail: sphere@ifrc.org; internet: www.sphereproject.org

10 | Vector control

10.1 Introduction

This chapter presents some of the important questions to consider when designing a project to prevent disease through vector control. The information it contains is adapted from *Disease Prevention through Vector Control* by Madeleine Thomson, published by Oxfam. Readers should refer to that and other publications for more information. Water and sanitation staff may implement vector-control activities, but this is a specialist field, and identifying vector-borne disease problems and designing an appropriate response needs advice from experts. See section 10.3.2 on roles and responsibilities. Methods of controlling vectors, particularly mosquitoes and flies, through general measures related to water supply and sanitation may be found in the relevant chapters of this book.

10.1.1 Vector-borne disease in emergencies

The control of vector-borne disease is a major priority in many emergency situations. Malaria is a significant cause of death in malaria-prevalent zones, and the risk of epidemics makes its control one of the public-health priorities for emergency situations in those areas. Numerous other vector-borne diseases, such as louse-borne typhus and yellow fever, may pose a health risk in specific areas and circumstances.

There are several reasons why people affected by disasters may be particularly at risk from vector-borne disease. They may lack previous exposure and immunity to the particular strain of vector-borne disease prevalent in the settlement area, such as malaria. They may have fled through an area infested with certain insect vectors, such as tsetse flies, the vectors of trypanosomiasis, or sleeping sickness. Displaced people or refugees may be forced to settle on land that local people avoid because of the prevalence of insect vectors, such as blackflies, the vectors of onchocerciasis, or river blindness. They may have lost their livestock, in which case insects that normally bite both humans and animals will feed more on humans. They may live in crowded and unhygienic conditions, where certain vector populations may dramatically increase, and lack of water for personal hygiene may make the problem worse; body lice, which may transmit relapsing fever, are an example of this type of problem. People affected by disasters may suffer acute stress, which may worsen sickness and which may be a factor in a cycle of malnutrition–infection–malnutrition. They may suffer from malnutrition, intestinal parasites, or blood loss due to injury, so making malaria more severe. Finally, national vector-control programmes may break down, or local resources may be inadequate to cope with the problem.

Measures to reduce morbidity and mortality due to vector-borne disease in an emergency must include other preventive and curative health measures and appropriate site selection and organisation, as well as measures to control vectors.

10.1.2 Definition of nuisance pests and vectors

It is important to distinguish between animals that are a nuisance and those that are mechanical and/or biological vectors. Most vectors of disease are also nuisance pests.

Nuisance pests

Pests such as rats or bedbugs become a nuisance when they are present in large numbers. Control programmes aim to reduce their numbers and/or reduce pest–human contact.

Mechanical vectors

These vectors, for example, houseflies, transmit pathogens by carrying them on their feet or mouth-parts. Control measures may aim to reduce the vector population, and to reduce the opportunities for disease transmission, for instance by ensuring that foodstuffs are covered.

Biological vectors

These vectors transmit a parasite or virus which must spend part of its life-cycle in the vector in order to mature to an infective stage capable of being transmitted to its human host. The parasite or virus is taken from and given to animal or human hosts when the vector takes a blood meal. Examples include mosquitoes, transmitting a number of parasitic and viral diseases, and tsetse flies, mites, ticks, and fleas. Biological vectors may be a serious threat to health even when their numbers are relatively low.

10.1.3 Controlling vector-borne disease: factors to consider

Careful consideration is needed before deciding on a strategy for controlling vector-borne disease. Some of the factors to consider include the following.

Diagnosis and epidemiological data
Data should be collected to help to answer the following questions:

- Who is infected: adults, children, men, women, new arrivals, established residents? This information may show where and when transmission is occurring, and who is most at risk. Such data should also be collected for the area surrounding the emergency settlement, to assess the vector-borne disease risk before disease outbreaks occur.
- Where do the infected people live and work? If the disease occurrence is localised, the control measures may be localised too, so that the control effort has maximum effect, and costs are kept down.

Identification and monitoring of vectors
Vectors present within and around the emergency settlement should be identified, and their geographic distribution mapped. This may be done using simple reference texts, or may need the help of a vector specialist. Once identified, vectors should be monitored. This is easier with pests, because the more there are, the more of a nuisance they are. With vector species, the disease risk is not necessarily in proportion to their numbers, and it is necessary to identify when and where they are biting, where and when they breed, and where they rest. Some of this information is gathered by trapping and identifying insects. Indirect indicators, such as rainfall data, can also be useful for predicting changes in numbers and distribution of insects.

Control in the acute phase
In the acute phase of an emergency, control of vector-borne disease may not be a priority, compared with provision of minimum water supplies and excreta-disposal facilities. In general, strategies for controlling vector-borne disease are planned and implemented over a longer period of time. But in some situations, the incidence of vector-borne disease may reach epidemic levels and justifies an emergency intervention. Such an intervention, commonly involving high-impact spraying to reduce insect numbers, should be seen as a short-term measure, complementing other control measures. The intervention is likely to be more appropriate and more effective if preparations can be made beforehand to ensure that the vector problem has been adequately investigated, that the correct insecticide and equipment are available, and that training is carried out.

Social and economic factors
In addition to epidemiological and entomological information, there are cultural factors that need to be taken into account during the planning stage. For instance, purdah may mean that body dusting of women for lice control is unacceptable. Poverty among the affected people may encourage them to sell bed-nets, or exchange them for other goods they may need.

Hygiene promotion

Hygiene promotion is an important tool for understanding these factors and also for encouraging the active involvement of the affected people in the control programme, and their acceptance of it. For instance, if people have concerns about the health effects of household insecticide spraying, they may wash it off the walls of their shelters or refuse entry to spraying teams. When carrying out rat control with poison baits, it is vital to discuss with people the location of the bait traps and ensure that they are aware of the possible risk to children and domestic animals.

Choice of insecticide

The choice of insecticide for a chemical control programme will be determined by a number of factors, including its ability to kill the target vector; availability and registration in the country; formulation for a particular application method; safety to humans and the environment; and cost. *The use of inappropriate insecticides is not only wasteful of precious resources, but may be hazardous too.*

Monitoring the project

Careful monitoring of the control project is required to verify its impact and ensure its continued effectiveness. Vector-control strategies may fail because of poor coverage and application practice. Unless monitored, these problems may not be noticed for some time, and the project may fail. Monitoring information should be gathered from the project activities and from the health information system. See the Sphere Project Minimum Standard for Vector Control for possible indicators to use for monitoring.

Justifying the control project

As with other aspects of water supply and sanitation in emergencies, vector-control programmes should be carried out in the context of local and national conditions, which have to be taken into account. Justification for specific vector-control activities may include the following.

- Control is part of the national health strategy in the host country.
- The control project is to be extended to the host community.
- The level of disease in the disaster-affected population is greater than in the host community.
- There is a risk of epidemics.
- Disease or drug resistance may spread from the disaster-affected community to the host community.
- Disease or drug resistance may spread from a displaced community to their home area on repatriation.

10.2 Assessment for strategies to control vector-borne disease

10.2.1 Key questions

These key questions should be answered when considering a control strategy for vector-borne disease:

- Is the vector-borne disease or the threat of vector-borne disease important in relation to other health problems at this stage of the emergency?
- Is the disease being transmitted in or around the emergency settlement?
- Are vector-control measures likely to have an effect? (Vector control is just one possible measure for controlling vector-borne disease. Others include personal protection, treatment with drugs, and prevention by the use of drugs.)

If the answer to the first three questions is 'yes', then the fourth question to answer is:

- What is the most effective vector-control strategy to adopt, as part of the disease-control project?

10.2.2 Assessing the relative importance of vector control

Although vector control may not always be a priority during the first phase of an emergency, it should be carried out whenever any of the following conditions applies.

- The actual or threatened mortality rate from the disease is high, and transmission is likely to occur in the emergency settlement: for instance where large numbers of non-immune people are arriving in an area where falciparum (cerebral) malaria is prevalent.
- There is a threat of an epidemic, and the control measure is relatively simple. For example, louse-borne diseases may reach epidemic proportions after some months, but mass delousing at reception centres and during registration can greatly reduce this risk.
- There is a vector-borne epidemic, such as dengue haemorrhagic fever, in the locality which can result in a high mortality rate.

During later phases, the need for specific vector-control activities should be assessed on the basis of the threat of morbidity, mortality, and nuisance value of the particular animal or insect.

10.2.3 Assessing the threat of morbidity and mortality

The main factors influencing the threat of morbidity and mortality due to vector-borne disease are the following:

- immune status of the population
- current health status of the population

- virulence of virus or parasite of concern
- prevalence of the disease vector in the area and potential for breeding
- availability and effectiveness of preventive and curative treatment.

10.2.4 Assessing where transmission is taking place

People may be infected before they arrive at the settlement, or they may be infected when they visit other places. Unless transmission is taking place within the emergency settlement, vector-control efforts will have little effect, so it is important to establish just where and when transmission occurs. It is necessary to know about the incubation period of the disease and people's movements, to be sure whether transmission is occurring inside or outside the settlement. You may need to gather this information by carrying out a survey of infected people, because routine health-centre data normally do not provide enough detail. Some knowledge of epidemiology and the important features of the diseases of concern is necessary for this assessment, and it may be necessary to call for expert assistance from government or WHO.

10.2.5 Assessing the likely effect of vector-control measures

It is not always the case that controlling vectors will have a significant impact on the transmission of disease, or that other measures such as personal protection will not be more cost-effective. Careful consideration of the short-term and long-term implications of the different options should be undertaken before a choice of control method or methods is made. This needs to be done in collaboration with staff working in health and other sectors.

10.2.6 Choosing a control strategy

There are often several different strategies that might be adopted to control disease transmission by a particular vector. For instance, possible malaria-control strategies might include modifying or destroying mosquito breeding sites, residual spraying with insecticide, or providing insecticide-treated bed-nets for personal protection. The option (or options) chosen should be cost-effective, should produce the desired impact within the required time, and should be acceptable in terms of conforming to national programmes, environmental standards, and the needs of the affected community.

10.3 Planning a vector-control strategy

10.3.1 Assessment and monitoring tools

Maps
A map should be made of the emergency settlement and the land within a radius of 2km around it, on a scale of 1:5000, showing sites that may be breeding

grounds for insect vectors and rodent pests. This map should be used to record action taken to treat or destroy breeding sites, and it should be updated regularly.

Satellite data can produce high-resolution images with information on rainfall and plant cover. These can provide useful information for assessing or predicting vector-breeding sites.

Pest and vector surveys

A vector specialist may carry out surveys to determine which species of insect or rodent pest and vector are present. Such surveys should be carried out regularly throughout the transmission season, and the results should be recorded on simple record sheets.

Surveys may involve active searches for insects and rodents, and the use of bait or light traps, or the capture or counting of insects feeding on humans or animals, to monitor the abundance, distribution, and habits of the vector or pest.

People from the disaster-affected community may be involved in the surveys, and are usually well informed about nuisance pests.

Using epidemiological information

As mentioned above, routine clinical data are not usually reliable or detailed enough to assess and monitor vector-borne disease problems and prevention activities; small sample surveys are therefore often needed. Most diseases vary seasonally, so surveys should be carried out throughout the year, to obtain up-to-date information in time to react to seasonal disease problems. Information gathered in such surveys includes recent and current occurrence of vector-borne disease and parasite counts for malaria.

10.3.2 Roles and responsibilities

Host governments

National control strategies in many countries affected by disasters are commonly affected by shortages of funds, personnel, and transport, if they function at all. Nevertheless, the appropriate government department should be consulted before setting up a specific control project, particularly if it involves the use of pesticides. The host government may be able to provide important information on the vector and disease patterns, advise on possible resistance, and grant licences for the use and import of chemicals if necessary.

Where there is an existing vertical national programme for the control of a specific disease, such as malaria, government resources may be quickly mobilised to deal with an outbreak.

International organisations

The WHO may be able to provide specialist advice, equipment, and insecticides, if requested, through the Ministry of Health of the host government. Other international organisations such as the UNHCR and ICRC may also be able to assist.

NGOs

NGOs may be involved in some or all of the following: providing technical expertise and technical support; funding all or part of a programme; and running a vector-control programme.

Vector specialists

A vector specialist, usually an entomologist, may be needed, to help to identify vector problems and design a control strategy. Consult local expertise first, if available. If not, it may be necessary to recruit a short-term consultant from an organisation with expertise in vector control. The tasks of a vector specialist are as follows.

To predict the likely vector problems. Take advice from a vector specialist on the location of the emergency settlement, and when assessing likely needs for vector control.

To identify the vector. This is particularly important for mosquitoes, of which many species exist, with varied disease significance.

To locate the breeding sites of the vector. This may be the most important function of the vector specialist, who may then be able to train others in recognising vector habitats.

To test the susceptibility of vectors to insecticide. This may be done in the field, or by sending captured insects to a laboratory.

To help to design the control programme and train the vector-control supervisors.

Further reading

D.C. Chavasse and H.H. Yap (1997) *Chemical Methods for the Control of Vectors and Pests of Public Health Importance*, WHO/CTD/WHOPES/97.2, Geneva: World Health Organisation

G. Sabatinelli (1997) *Vector and Pest Control in Refugee Situations*, Geneva: PTSS/UNHCR and Rome: ISS/WHO

Sphere Project (1999, forthcoming) *Humanitarian Charter and Minimum Standards in Disaster Response*, Chapter 2, section 4, 'Vector Control', published in Geneva by the Steering Committee for Humanitarian Response (SCHR) and Interaction; e-mail: sphere@ifrc.org; internet: *www.sphereproject.org*

M. Thomson (1995) *Disease Prevention through Vector Control: Guidelines for Relief Organisations*, Oxford: Oxfam

11 | Managing solid waste

11.1 Introduction

Solid waste is produced by household activities such as food preparation, by commercial activity (markets, workshops, etc.), by health centres and other central services, and occasionally as a direct result of war or natural disaster. When deciding how to deal with solid waste, it is important to consider how much of a health risk it poses and how acute the risk is; what other problems it causes, such as blocking roads and drains or creating a depressing environment; what is the scale of the problem, i.e. how much waste is involved; what is the nature of the solid waste; whether the problem is a short-term one or whether it will need continuing attention; whose responsibility it should be to tackle the problem; what resources will be needed for the work; and what are the technical and organisational options for storage, collection, transport, and disposal. See assessment questions in Chapter 2.

11.2 Health risks of solid waste

Solid waste rarely poses a direct threat to health, and in most emergencies it is not a major priority in the first response. Solid waste from household activities (domestic refuse) may contain faeces (particularly children's faeces), and so may pose some direct risk to health, but most of the risks are secondary. Domestic refuse and market refuse may attract rats and dogs and may therefore be a breeding ground for flies. Leachate from solid waste under wet conditions may pollute water sources and run into shelters.

11.3 Managing solid waste

Most of the information in this section concerns household refuse. Transporting and disposing of commercial wastes is managed in a similar way, but organisation of collection from commercial areas and cleaning such areas needs special attention. See section 11.3.7.

11.3.1 Quantities and composition

The most important source of solid waste in emergency settlements is activity connected with food preparation by families. The amount of waste produced and its composition are extremely variable; they depend very much on what food is prepared and in what form it is supplied or bought. As a rough guide, each person may produce between 0.5 and 1.0 litres of refuse each day, which may have a moisture content between 10 and 60 per cent and an organic content (weight for weight of dry matter) of 25 to 35 per cent. There are likely to be seasonal variations and changes over time, as activities in the emergency settlement develop. The only way to get reliable information on the waste to be dealt with is to look closely at it, weigh it, and see what it is composed of.

In camps of Iraqi Kurdish refugees in Turkey in 1991, army rations were supplied, wrapped in several layers of plastic and containing several dishes that people would not eat, so a huge amount of refuse was produced. In many African refugee camps, people are given dry rations of cereal, pulses, and oil, with very little waste produced in the preparation. What little waste that is produced can easily be dealt with by burying it in small pits near the shelters. Whatever rations are given, many refugees also buy or exchange food. For instance, in Rwandan refugee camps in Zaire, many refugees exchanged maize for bananas and sugar cane, and preparing these foods produced large volumes of waste. Where refugees have livestock, food wastes may be fed to them, or wastes may be put on gardens, leaving very little inorganic waste to dispose of.

11.3.2 Solid-waste management project

During the first days of an emergency, disposing of household refuse is unlikely to be a priority. If it is an urgent problem, it is unrealistic to expect people affected by the disaster to take responsibility for it: an agency should take on this task. However, long-term collection and disposal of refuse is an expensive activity which is difficult to sustain. Where possible, look for ways of reducing the amount of refuse produced, or of encouraging and enabling safe recycling or disposal within the settlement. It may be possible to privatise waste collection and disposal, provided that minimum standards of operation are guaranteed by the contract for the work. In an urban situation, a municipal authority may be responsible.

Hygiene promotion

The project involves storage of refuse before collection, collection, transport, and disposal. At each of these stages there are possible options, and these will be discussed below. The way in which responsibility for these activities is shared between the agency and the disaster-affected community may change over time; it will depend to some extent on the policy of the agency. Most solid-waste management programmes depend on the participation of the population concerned for placing their refuse in containers provided, or burying it, where appropriate. Parents and children should be made aware of the dangers of playing with or recycling medical wastes.

Staff needs

Staff numbers needed for running a domestic-refuse collection and disposal project depend on the quantities of refuse produced, the size of the camp, and factors such as access. For an example, in Kahindo Rwandan refugee camp near Goma, 25 staff were employed to collect and dispose of approximately 350 m³ of refuse per week from 110,000 refugees. Staff employed to handle refuse should be provided with overalls, boots, and gloves. Workers burning refuse or handling dusty waste should have protective masks. At disposal sites there should be water and soap available for washing hands and faces, and for washing vehicles if they have been transporting hazardous waste such as latrine sludge.

11.3.3 Disposal on site

Where possible, this is the preferred method, because it involves no collection vehicles, disposal site, or staff. Individual families or groups of families can dig shallow pits near their shelters and throw their refuse in. They should be discouraged from burning it, because of the smoke created in the camp, but they should be encouraged to scatter ashes from cooking fires on the refuse heap regularly, to reduce fly breeding. This is common practice in many villages around the world. Where rats are a serious problem, this is not a suitable method, unless the refuse contains very little food waste.

In many refugee camps, people cultivate gardens, even when space is short. Household refuse contains valuable organic matter and nutrients, which people may use to increase the fertility of the soil. Composting is unlikely to work at the household level because of the small quantity of refuse produced, but it may be successful if several families combine their waste.

11.3.4 Storage

If household waste is to be collected and disposed of centrally, it has to be stored until the time of collection. This storage time should be kept to a minimum, particularly in humid tropical conditions. Ideally people should be able to throw out their refuse daily, or twice weekly at least.

Household containers: The easiest way for families to dispose of refuse is to have a container in each shelter which can be taken to a nearby point for collection. In the early days of an emergency, plastic refuse sacks may be distributed, particularly if a large amount of refuse is being produced. Unless adequate shelter material is also provided, however, these sacks are likely to be used for building shelters. It would be better to provide metal containers with lids to keep rats away, but these are expensive to buy and transport and would probably be used for food storage (particularly if there is a rat problem), rather than refuse. However, it is an option to be considered at a later stage, when local production of containers is possible.

Small collective containers: These are roadside containers into which people throw their refuse for collection. The most common option is 200-litre oil drums, whole or cut in half, with drainage holes near the bottom and handles for lifting. If possible they should have lids to discourage flies. It is recommended to provide one drum per 10 families for a twice-weekly collection. This may not be possible in many situations, because drums are often expensive and difficult to find in large numbers. An alternative may be to use nylon bags of the sort sometimes used to deliver sand to small building sites. Usually one cubic metre in capacity, they require several people to lift them on to a truck or cart when full.

Waste-collection depots: A number of refuse-collection depots may be built around the settlement from masonry or timber, where people can throw refuse. Another alternative is to leave skips or trailers dispersed around the settlement for this purpose. These containers should have high sides to maximise the volume of refuse that can be carried to the disposal site, and covers to keep off rain and flies.

The type of collection system that is possible and the degree to which it operates successfully will depend very much on the participation of the users of the system, and their willingness to make it work. This makes consultation very important, to find out the most suitable system to use, and to encourage people to share responsibility for its success.

11.3.5 Collection and transport

In general, aim to empty refuse depots daily, and small containers such as oil drums twice weekly. The options for transport are hand-carts, animal carts, small powered trailers, skip trucks/tractor and trailers, or ordinary trucks. Aim for the most simple and least expensive alternative.

Hand-carts: These may already be locally available or can be made specially, either with open high sides or with bins, to carry 300–500 litres. Each operator can serve about 500 families. Hand-carts are limited to a radius of about 1km, so could not serve a camp of more than 10,000 or 20,000 people, unless they were used in a large camp for primary collection and off-loading into larger vehicles for transport to a more distant disposal site. They are unsuitable for hilly ground. A collection system based on hand-carts may easily be privatised or managed by the refugees themselves.

Animal carts: Donkey, horse, or ox carts may carry up to 2m^3, can operate over a radius of 3km, and may be used in more hilly areas. They are more expensive to construct, however, and they depend on there being draught animals available and a local tradition of using them.

Small powered vehicles: In some countries, trailers pulled by small powered units like horticultural cultivators are used for local transport. They may be adapted for refuse collection and transport over a 5km radius, though this depends on the power and speed of the tractor unit. They can manage quite steep hills and can be used on small tracks where larger vehicles cannot go. They do need more intensive maintenance and external support than hand-carts and animal carts, but may still be run under community or private management.

Skip trucks and tractors with trailers: These allow large waste containers to be left in the camp, which can then be towed away or carried away when full, to be replaced with an empty one. It is expensive to hire or buy this equipment, and is not really worth it except in a large camp (more than about 50,000 people) which is likely to remain for some time. Trailers and skips should be provided with high sides to increase the volume of refuse collected and transported, and preferably should be fitted with a cover, to prevent rain entering and to discourage flies and smell.

Ordinary trucks: In most situations it is possible to hire or buy flatbed trucks, with a capacity ranging from 3 to 7 tonnes, which can be fitted with high sides for refuse collection. This is often the most rapid way to get a system going. These trucks can be used for collecting from roadside containers, direct from householders bringing their refuse to the road at specified times, or from depots in the camp. Five or so workers with hand tools are needed for loading and off-loading each truck, if collecting from depots or from roadside oil drums.

11.3.6 Centralised disposal

The options are burying, burning (or a combination of the two), composting, and recycling.

Burying: A site is needed at least 500 metres away and downwind from living areas, 50 metres away from water points, and downhill from ground-water sources. It may be possible to use natural or man-made pits, to dig trenches by machine and then back-fill when full, or to heap the refuse on a flat site. Ensure that the bottom of the pit, or the ground level of a flat tipping site, is at least 1.5m above the water table. Ensure that leachate which drains from the tip does not pollute surface water and ground-water. Dispose of leachate in a soakaway pit if possible. Refuse should be covered every day, or burned to keep off flies, rats, and dogs. Burning also helps to reduce the volume of waste. After six months or so, the refuse may be dug out for use as compost.

Burning: Where the waste has a high organic content (paper, food wastes, etc.) and a low moisture content, it may be burned to reduce its volume by at least 70 per cent, if space for tipping is limited. Household and market waste is too bulky to be burned in incinerators and is usually simply burned slowly in heaps. This creates air pollution and an additional hazard for workers; it should be avoided if possible, except for hazardous waste from hospitals, which should be burned in efficient incinerators. See section 11.4.

Where space for burying refuse is scarce, a combination of burying and burning may be used to reduce the volume to be buried.

Composting: The simplest form of composting (aerobic decomposition) is to leave the refuse in pits or heaps for several months, where eventually it will decompose and become safe to handle and useful for improving soil fertility. However, composting proper involves very intense microbial activity which heats the material, kills off pathogens (disease-causing organisms), and decomposes it in a matter of weeks. This requires careful management to ensure that the waste has the right moisture content and the right ration of carbon to nitrogen, and is provided with enough air for the process to work. This is most effectively managed centrally, to control the operation and ensure that the right quantities of waste are available. Refuse may also be composted with the contents of latrines, though this requires more attention and better-trained and equipped staff. Again, the simplest method is to leave the material for at least a year to decompose slowly.

Recycling: There is generally very little waste useful for recycling in refugee camps. Resources are generally very scarce, and people use every piece of scrap metal, paper, and plastic available. A certain amount of unofficial recycling is done by people scavenging in waste bins and depots. Where cooking fuel is short, people may burn dried plant wastes such as maize stalks for cooking. This is very time-consuming, because this material burns very fast, and the fire needs to be fed continuously. There is great potential for using burnable material in waste for making fuel briquettes, though this has rarely been done in practice in emergency settlements.

11.3.7 Commercial waste

Markets, shops, and services like hairdressers very quickly spring up in refugee camps and in towns hit by disasters. The wastes produced may be very similar to household refuse and depend on what goods are available and how much trading goes on. Trading is usually organised by a committee or local authority, who should be encouraged to take responsibility for waste management at the market, raising money from traders if necessary to pay for cleaners. Whenever possible, the wastes should be buried on site and covered over each day. If this is not possible, the market should be included in the general waste-collection schedule, on a daily basis if possible.

Slaughterhouse waste may need special treatment and special facilities to deal with the liquid wastes produced, and to ensure that slaughtering is carried out in hygienic conditions.

11.4 Waste from health centres

Health centres, feeding centres, and orphanages produce waste which may be of particular risk to health and should be given special attention. Waste may include soiled and infectious dressings, and used needles and surgical tools. This type of waste should be disposed of within the boundary of the health centre whenever possible, and is the responsibility of the agency running the centre. Waste should be collected in covered containers, emptied regularly by staff. Needles, blades, and other sharps should be collected in special containers bought for the purpose or made from empty drinks tins or bottles. The best method of disposal is incineration, to kill pathogens and reduce the volume of waste for subsequent burying. Incinerators are designed and built to achieve high temperatures and complete combustion of waste material, and they require correct operation to ensure that they perform as intended. Fuel may be required to achieve the required temperature. Simply burning waste in an open fire is not sufficient for dangerous waste, since sharps may not be destroyed, even at high temperatures. If the incinerator is built over a pit, the ashes drop straight into it without having to be handled. The waste should be burned at least once each day by a staff member who is given specific responsibility for this.

Non-contaminated waste should be kept and disposed of separately from contaminated waste, so that the volume of waste to be disposed of by incineration or other special means is kept to a minimum. Food and other wastes with a high moisture content should be buried in a separate fly-proof pit. On no account should dangerous hospital waste be mixed with waste for the general collection, and special care is needed to prevent children from taking dangerous waste to make toys, fishing hooks, etc.

11.5 Dead bodies

Dead bodies are rarely the health hazard that they are often feared to be, and only in rare circumstances should they be considered as a solid-waste problem. They should, as far as possible, be handled and buried or cremated by the families of the dead people, unless this is no longer the tradition, as in much of the Western world, where specialist services may exist. Most traditional practices are safe and hygienic under normal circumstances. It is very important to be aware of customary practices relating to funerals, burial or cremation, and mourning, and their significance for the well-being of people in disasters.

However, when people have died of cholera, typhus, or plague, their bodies need special attention, to contain infective stools and vomit, lice, and fleas before burial. In crowded camps and particularly when there may be many people dying each day, an agency may have to take responsibility for the safe handling and disposal of corpses. In extreme cases, as in the cholera epidemic in the Rwandan refugee camps in Goma in 1994, this may have to be done on a mass scale with mechanical equipment. This is a very stressful job for the workers involved, who may need special support to help them to deal with it. Whatever the situation, however, every effort should be made to allow the families of the deceased to look after their dead in the way they normally do.

Where dead bodies find their way into water sources or fishing areas, it is important to recover the corpses, to avoid any possible health risk and to reduce people's fears. It is also important to retrieve bodies for identification and for funerals to be held. The same is true where people have died in earthquakes or hurricanes and their bodies are trapped under damaged buildings.

Further reading

J. Davis and R. Lambert (1996) *Engineering in Emergencies: A practical guide for relief workers,* chapter 8, London: RedR/IT Publications

I. Lardinois and A. van de Klundert (eds.) (1993) *Organic Waste: Options for small-scale resource recovery,* Amsterdam: TOOL/Gouda: WASTE Consultants

MSF (1992) *Public Health Engineer for Emergency Situation,* first edition, Paris: Médicins sans Frontières

Sphere Project (1999, forthcoming) *Humanitarian Charter and Minimum Standards in Disaster Response,* Chapter 2, section 5, 'Solid Waste Disposal', published in Geneva by the Steering Committee for Humanitarian Response (SCHR) and Interaction; e-mail: sphere@ifrc.org; internet: *www.sphereproject.org*

UNHCS (1989) *Solid Waste Management in Low-income Housing Projects: The scope for community participation,* Nairobi: UNHCS (Habitat)

K. Wilson and B. Harrell-Bond (1990) 'Dealing with dying', *Refugee Participation Network Newsletter* No 9, August 1990, Oxford: Refugee Studies Programme

12 | Drainage

12.1 Introduction

Surface water in and near emergency settlements may come from household and water-point waste water, leaking water pipes, latrines, and sewers, rain water, and rising floodwater. The main health problems associated with this water in emergencies are contamination of water supplies and the living environment, damage to latrines and shelters, the creation of vector-breeding sites, and the risk of drowning. On the other hand, surface water in and near the settlement may provide benefits in terms of health and facilities for people to wash themselves, their utensils, and their clothes. You should appraise the benefits and risks when deciding whether or not to drain or fill such water bodies.

This chapter addresses small-scale drainage problems and activities. The most effective way to avoid large-scale drainage problems is to give careful thought to the choice and lay-out of the emergency settlement (see Chapter 6).

12.2 Waste water

Waste water is generated from several sources, including the following:

- excreta disposal;
- personal bathing/laundry/cooking/washing of utensils (sullage);
- spillage and leaks from water-collection facilities.

In all of these instances, the main factors to consider are soil conditions and the provision of facilities to enhance health. It is important also to involve the community in decisions about how the facilities will be used.

12.2.1 Excreta disposal

The safe disposal of waste water from excreta disposal is of major significance to health, because this water carries many pathogens. If latrines are used intensively or used for bathing as well as for toilets, and the liquid load added exceeds their capacity to filter into the ground, they will fill and may overflow. On some sloping sites on fractured rock, liquid may seep from latrines to the surface farther down the slope. Damage to infrastructure as a result of war or natural disaster may cause sewers to break or sewage pumps to break down, so allowing sewage to spill on to the surface.

For cases where small volumes of waste water are affected by high faecal contamination, sprinkling with sand and quicklime to absorb and disinfect the waste water and control flies is often the most practical short-term measure to take while the problem that is creating the leakage is tackled. Where large volumes of sewage are spilled, pumping into tankers or back into operating sewers or storm drains may be necessary to clear the contamination from public areas. When planning repairs to existing water supplies, it is important to ensure that drains and sewers are clear and operating, to avoid creating waste-water leakages.

12.2.2 Sullage and spillage

Sullage
The waste water generated from activities such as bathing, cooking, and laundry is often termed **sullage**. Although it poses a lower level of health risk than waste water from excreta disposal, it does need to be disposed of properly. The number of pathogens in the waste water itself is usually low, but the water may provide a rich breeding ground for flies and mosquitoes. Also it can smell very unpleasant. If this waste water is produced at the home and scattered on the ground, as is common practice in many poor tropical areas, there is unlikely to be any significant impact on health. However, if a large quantity of sullage is emptied into drains or produced at a central communal facility, it needs careful disposal to avoid health risks and other problems.

In general, avoid trying to dispose of waste water by filtration into the ground; this applies particularly to waste water from washing facilities, because soap, sand, and grease will eventually cause blockages and clog the soil surface, even when traps for grease and sand are used. It is usually more successful to site facilities so that water can be moved away quickly by gravity in open drains, and then channelled into natural water courses (check the final destination of this flow, to avoid causing problems downstream); or it can be used for irrigation. In most camps there is a need for extra supplies of fresh food, and it is usually possible to arrange for someone to manage a garden, using waste water for irrigation. Care is needed, however, to avoid large amounts of water being drawn deliberately for watering the garden. During rainy periods, the flow should be directed into the settlement's main drainage system.

If there is no option but to dispose of the waste water into the soil (for instance, within a cholera isolation and treatment centre), install a large-capacity trap for grease and sand in line before the soakaway or infiltration drains; build the soakaway so that it can easily be uncovered for unblocking and cleaning; and make provision for expanding the soakaway, building a second one in parallel, or further pits in series. Careful and frequent maintenance is very important. Carry out percolation tests to quantify infiltration capacities for the design of soakaway pits and trenches. In some instances it may be necessary to augur through a relatively impermeable layer to get through to a more permeable layer. Consider the use of a hand auger for small quantities of water.

The drainage facilities should be designed to cope with the maximum expected production of waste water. This tends to increase as settlements become more established and people use more water and do more washing. In the early stages, therefore, some over-design may be needed.

Spillage from water-collection facilities
Clean water spilled during water collection should be directed away from water-collection points, to provide people with a serviceable area to collect water from, and to avoid producing vector-breeding sites. The provision under the distribution points of suitable materials such as gravel, or sand on a plastic membrane, would be an appropriate first-phase activity. Later, if required, the system could be upgraded by using either concrete or bricks, laid in a herringbone fashion.

If water is drained separately from water-collection points, it may be used for watering animals; drinking troughs may be built for this purpose, at least 30 metres from the water point. The areas around drinking troughs pose drainage problems too, and these need to be dealt with, in co-operation with the animals' owners.

Taps should be regularly maintained to reduce leaks. Water users could be involved in tap maintenance, given sufficient training, tools and spare parts.

12.3 Storm water

Storm water is generated from several sources, including the following:

- rain-water run-off;
- flooding of surface-water sources such as rivers and lakes after rain;
- water-logging due to raising of water table.

In flood-prone regions, it is critical to determine the extent and duration of flooding during the initial assessment, and to plan accordingly.

12.3.1 Rain-water run-off

The main concern here is to ensure that rain-water run-off during periods of rain does not flood shelters, pollute water sources, or damage latrines. The last point is especially important, because rain-water that seeps into latrines down the edge of a pit without a lining can be very destabilising and could cause soil to collapse in the pit and fill it prematurely. This can be best avoided by raising the latrine slab at least 150mm above the ground, using a mound of well-compacted soil around the latrine to deflect water away from the pit, and digging a diversion drain around the latrine to keep water away from the pit edges. Another concern, at the early stages of an emergency, is faeces on the ground, which may be washed down slopes towards water sources or living areas.

It is best if a settlement can be located on sloping ground so that it will self-drain. Then water run-off can be dealt with by building diversion channels to direct water away from vulnerable areas. These channels rarely have to be purpose-designed and protected, but in some countries where rainfall is very high this may be necessary. If so, channels should be designed and constructed of sufficient dimensions and with slopes slight enough to reduce their erosion. Where the channel changes direction, slope, or width, it may need strengthening with concrete blocks or wood, otherwise scouring and collapse may occur. The channels will need to be maintained and occasionally repaired, to ensure that debris is cleaned out, and thus to minimise the risk of the channel being blocked and overflowing.

It is important to check that new construction work does not cause drainage problems. For instance, new roads can dam water unless they are designed and built correctly.

12.3.2 Flooding of surface-water sources after rain

Again this will occur most during seasons of heavy rain. When selecting sites, avoid flood plains of rivers and areas below high-level points of lakes. Floods can cause physical damage to structures and encourage mosquitoes to breed. Look for signs in vegetation and debris, and use local knowledge to find out what is flood level. Seasonal springs may also cause local drainage problems.

12.3.3 Water-logging due to high water table

Flat land or areas of land in a natural bowl are prone to water-logging. Where possible, the highest seasonal-level water table should be at least 3m below ground surface; this is very important for latrine-construction reasons. Settlements should never be located in marshy areas. Rocky and impermeable soils may also create flood-prone locations.

12.3.4 Drainage of existing surface-water sources

In some cases it may be useful to consider draining or back-filling existing surface-water sources if they constitute a risk in terms of potential vector-breeding sites. Small water courses may be diverted, while stagnant standing bodies of water could perhaps be back-filled, using either mass labour or mechanical plant. However, as malaria-bearing mosquitoes have a dispersal range of up to 2km, it is rarely possible to drain all the surface-water sources within this distance of the settlement.

12.4 Community involvement

Where small-scale drainage works are necessary to protect latrines and shelters, and to avoid stagnant household and water-point waste water, it may be appropriate to involve the population concerned. Technical support and tools may then be needed, and this may be linked with a hygiene-promotion programme. It may also be necessary to provide information and alternatives if local water bodies pose health risks such as schistosomiasis, or hazards from consumption of the water.

Further reading

J. Davis and R. Lambert (1995) *Engineering in Emergencies: A practical guide for relief workers*, Chapter 8, London: RedR/IT Publications

MSF (1992) *Public Health Technician in Emergency Situation*, first edition, Chapter 2, Paris: Médecins sans Frontières

Sphere Project (1999, forthcoming) *Humanitarian Charter and Minimum Standards in Disaster Response*, Chapter 2, section 6, 'Drainage', published in Geneva by the Steering Committee for Humanitarian Response (SCHR) and Interaction; e-mail: sphere@ifrc.org; internet: *www.sphereproject.org*

WHO (1991) *Surface Water Drainage for Low-income Communities*, Geneva: World Health Organisation

Index

collaboration (participation) 101; drainage 183; empowerment 23–5; guidelines 147; hygiene promotion 100; long-term relationships 54; participation guidelines 147; resources checklist 32; transient, settlement 12; water supply 112, 114–15

communication methods 106

communications, and rapid response 45

community, local: *see* local community

community formation 22, 90; acute emergency phase 52; site design 95

community involvement: *see* collaboration

community organisation, checklist 32

composting 172, 173, 175, 176

concrete slabs, pit latrines 156

construction work management 82–3

consultation 26, 56; discussion groups 106, 108; equal opportunities 45; waste disposal 174; water distribution and access 132; *see also* collaboration

contamination, chemical 111

contamination source detection 40, 136

contingency planning 56–8

contingency stocks 74–5, 79

contractors 84, 118

cooking, waste water 180–1

crude mortality rate (CMR) 20

cultural factors: burial 95; insect control 165; latrine design 94, 97, 143, 146; water usage 96

dams 128

data: disaggregation 18; ground-water extraction 117–19; interpretation 43–4; quality 45; representative 41, 42; water distribution 114–15; *see also* information

data-recording system 66

data reliability: cross-checking 43; impact monitoring 63; indicator choice 65; interviews 41, 42; questionnaires 102; sampling 41

data sources: for evaluation 69; project monitoring 63

dead bodies, disposal 177–8

death: *see* mortality

decision-making: *see* collaboration

defecation: acute emergency phase 52; children 38, 101, 171; water protection 113; *see also* excreta disposal; latrines; toilets

defecation fields 151–3; staffing 148

demography, checklist 31–2

diagramming 43

diarrhoea 16, 106

disabled people: access 18; employment 82; toilets 104, 143

disaster, defined 15

discussion groups, representative 106, 108

disease: acute emergency phase 52; background level 21; excreta-related 16; health-related skills 24; increased prevalence causes 163–4; local 12; transmission 16–17, 99; urban displacement 13

disease, vector-borne: assessment strategies 167–8; checklist 36–7; epidemiology 165; excreta-disposal methods 36; prevalence 163–4; transmission location 168; *see also* vector control

disinfection: *see* chlorination; water treatment

displaced people 22

diversion channels 182

diversity: *see* cultural factors

domestic (household) visits 42

drainage 95; blockage by solid waste 37; checklist 38; community involvement 183; site characteristics impact 98; uncontrolled 131; waste water 179–81

draining water sources 183

elderly people: employment 82; toilets 143; water access 132

emergencies: stability 20; timescale 53–4; typology 11–15; *see also* contingency

employment: contracts 82; equality issues 82; local 27; sense of worth 81

empowerment *see* collaboration; consultation

endemic disease 21

entomologists 170

environmental degradation 28; site selection 91, 92; wood 155

environmental health: defined 15; disease checklist 31; risk 16–17, 92; *see also* disease; health

epidemic disease 21; checklist 31; disposal of bodies 178; insect control 165; monitoring 63

epidemiology 15, 169

equipment: choosing 61, 72–3; emergency stocks 74–5, 79; features 72–3; importing 76; international purchasing 75; labelling 79; local stocks 57–8; ownership 61; packs 73; rapid-reaction 73; re-use 61; regional purchasing 76; specification 74; storage 61, 79; suppliers 75–6

Escherichia coli 135

evaluation 67–8; external 70; information dissemination 70; information sources 69

excreta, waste water 180

excreta disposal: acute phase 12, 139, 150; checklist 35–6; difficult sites 161; habitual patterns 140; phased response 139–42; planning 94–5; preferred practices 35; as priority 138; roadside 12, 139; site characteristics 97; *see also* defecation; latrine; toilet

excreta-related disease 16

faecal contamination: *see* water contamination

family toilet (latrine) 140–1, 142, 146–7; cleanliness 145; latrine choice 159–60; maintenance 147; public t. comparison 140, 144–5; shallow 157–8; shared 147; staffing 148; *see also* latrine

field assessment: checklist 31–9; for evaluation information 69 ; guidelines 45–6; initial 45

field assessment techniques 39–43; choice 39; by experts 40; interviews 41–2; survey 40–1; technical assessment 39; visual 40

field logistics 77–9

filtration 120, 122

financial accountability 108

financial monitoring 51; *see also* accounting; budgets

flocculation 120–1

flooding 38, 181–2; defecation fields 151; diversion channels 182; *see also* drainage

fly control, latrines: pit 155, 159; pour-flush 160; VIP 160

focus groups 42

food preparation, solid waste from 172

frameworks 48, 48, 49–50

fuel availability 91

funeral rites 177, 178

goals 48, 49; *see also* objectives

government: agency integration 55 ; aid 23, 108; vector-control strategy 169

gravity flow 123, 129

grease-trap 181

ground-water: pit-latrine construction 154; monitoring 119; pit-latrine pollution 154–5; well 118–19

group work 107

hand-washing: hygiene promotion 101; importance 99; *see also* soap

handover 59–60; toilets 145–6

health: checklist 31–2; local population 27; *see also* disease; environmental h.

health centre: water supply 111, 128; water storage 128; *see also* medical waste

health data (HIS) 18, 20–2; reliability 21–2

host authorities, assistance 23

household visits 42

housing repairs, war damage 14

humanitarian agencies 23

hygiene, and disease 17, 99, 164; water quantity/quality balance 111–12

hygiene-practices assessment 101–2

hygiene promotion 23, 24, 98; checklist 33, 39–40; defecation fields 153; defined 100; education 100, 103; excreta disposal 140, 141; family toilets 146–7; information

sampling 40–1; representative 45
sanitary survey 40, 136
sanitation: on closedown 60–1; long-
term management 108; public-health
approach 18–22; rapid-response
equipment 73; short-term solutions
104; technical assessment 93
sanitation teams 150
schools, hygiene education 103
seasonal settlements 12
security: equipment storage 79; site
selection 90; *see also* safety
septic tanks 150
settlement: *see* camp; site
sewage spills 180
sewerage system adaptation 149–50
showers 132–3
site: access 58; assessment 92; closedown
60–1; draining 183; handover 59–60;
identification of, contingency
planning 58; physical characteristics
and service design 96–8; physical
considerations 90–1; *see also* camps
site location: disease 163–4; flood-prone
182; layout 96–8; self-draining 182;
service provision 96
site planning: burial 95; drainage 95;
excreta disposal 94–5; hygiene
promotion 95; solid-waste
management 95; vector control 95;
water supply 94
site selection 89–94; decision-making
93–4; procedure 91–2; ranking 92, 93;
requirements prioritisation 89–91, 92
slab-production workshop 156
slabs, pit latrines 155–6
slaughterhouse waste 177
slow-onset emergencies 22
slow sand filters 122
sludge accumulation 153
soakaways 175, 181
soap 33, 113; defecation fields 153; *see also*
hand washing
social diversity 25–26; *see also* children;
community formation; cultural
factors; disabled people; elderly
people; women

soil, waste water disposal 180–1
soil conditions: defecation fields 151; pit
latrines 154; waste water 179; well
construction 118–19
solar power pump 124
solid waste: collection 174–5;
commercial 176–7; disposal 37, 174,
175–6; faeces in 171; health risks 171;
management 95, 172–3; on-site
disposal 173; site characteristics 97;
storage 173–4
specification of equipment 74
Sphere standards: humanitarian
response 17, 18; toilet provision 140;
vector control 166; water quality 111
spillage disposal 181
stabilised emergency phase 20, 53
staff 80–4; for hygiene promotion
103–4; needs 80–1; pump operation
125–6; refugee 81–2; sanitation
development 147–8; women 115
staff input, site selection 93
staff management 80
statistical information: *see* data;
interviews; survey
stock management 77–8; buffer stock 79;
contingency 74–5, 79; field 78–9
storm water 181–3
stress 17, 164
sullage 180–1
supply continuity, water 115
supply management: *see* logistics
surface water 112, 116–17; protection 117;
sources 179
survey 39, 40–1; *see also* sanitary survey
system operation and maintenance 59

tankering 34, 114, 126–7
taps 131, 132
taste, water 119, 121, 122
testing water 134–6
toilet programme monitoring 149
toilets: access 138, 139, 143; construction
144; cultural factors 143, 146;
familiarity with 35; handing over
145–6; long-term target 141;
management 143; minimum

standards 17–18; planning 139; roadside 12; technical quality 144; water demands 111; *see also* defecation; excreta disposal; family toilets; latrine; public toilets; sanitation

training: contingency planning 57; equal opportunities 26; hygiene 107; hygiene outreach workers 104

transient settlements 12

transit centres 14

transport 76; equipment purchasing 75, 76; monitoring 77

trauma 25

trench latrines 152, 155, 158–9

turbidity 116, 119, 120–1, 134

typhoid 16

UN 19

urban area 13; contingency equipment 75; sewerage system 149–50

vector 164

vector-borne disease: *see* disease

vector control 37, 164–6, 168–70; effect assessment 168; monitoring 165; project justification 166; site impact 97; site planning 95; stagnant water 15; surveys 169

VIP latrine 160

vulnerability 15

wages: *see* pay

war damage 14

warehousing 79

washing (clothes) 131, 132

washing (personal) 36, 131, 132–3

waste *see* solid waste

waste water 133, 179–81

water: consumption levels 110–11; minimum requirements 113; minimum standards 17–18; pre-treatments 120; public-health approach 18–22; quality 111, 115–16, 134–5; quantity/quality trade-off 111–12; stagnant, vector control 15; *see also* ground water; surface water

water access 33, 110, 128–9, 132; security 84

water committee 102, 114, 133–4

water container 33, 131, 133; children 132, 133; priority action 113; size 132

water contamination 33; chemical 111; excreta 35, 113, 116; floods 14–15, 38; tests 134–6; waste burying 175

water distribution 128–31; consultation 132; design and installation 128–9; equipment 130–1; phased implementation 129–30; system implementation 114; tap siting 129; *see also* gravity flow; pumping

water-logging 182

water meters 131

water points, maintenance and repair 133–4

water sources 112, 115–19; ground 117–19; protection checklist 33; surface 116–17

water storage 127–8; chlorination 129; testing 135

water supply: acute phase 52; assessment checklist 33–4; and camp life-time 112; on closedown 60–1; community involvement 114–15; contingency equipment 57; continuity 115, 116–17; cultural aspects 96; local population 27, 34; long-term management 108; phased approach 113–14; planning 94; priority actions 113–14; rapid-response 73; roadside 12; sewerage system 149; site characteristics impact 96; site selection 91, 93; spillage 181; technical assessment 93; variation in, checklist 34

water treatment 112, 119–23; checklist 33; packs 123; phased approach 123; priority action 113; purpose 119; testing 134–6

well 118–19; *see also* ground water

women: access 18; decision participation 23, 26, 101, 106, 108; employment 81, 82; recruiting as staff 115; safety 18, 152; washing facilities 132; water carrying 131; workload 81

wood 91, 155